HOW

Help!

DO I
READ
THE?
BIBLE!

J.

A JESUS-CENTERED GUIDE J.

A JESUS-CENTERED GUIDE

HELP! HOW DO I READ THE BIBLE?

Copyright © 2018 Group Publishing, Inc./0000 0001 0362 4853

Lifetree™ is an imprint of Group Publishing, Inc.

Visit our website: group.com

Written by Mikal Keefer

Scripture quotations are taken from the Holy Bible, New Living Translation, copyright © 1996, 2004, 2007, 2013, 2015 by Tyndale House Foundation. Used by permission of Tyndale House Publishers, Inc., Carol Stream, Illinois 60188. All rights reserved.

Library of Congress Cataloging-in-Publication Data

Names: Group Publishing.
Title: Help! How do I read the Bible?
Description: First American paperback [edition]. | Loveland, Colorado : Group
  Publishing, Inc., 2018. | Series: A Jesus-centered guide
Identifiers: LCCN 2017052349 (print) | LCCN 2017055285 (ebook) | ISBN
  9781470753238 (ePub) | ISBN 9781470753221 (pbk.)
Subjects: LCSH: Bible--Reading.
Classification: LCC BS617 (ebook) | LCC BS617 .H455 2018 (print) | DDC
  220.6/1--dc23
LC record available at https://lccn.loc.gov/2017052349

ISBN: 978-1-4707-5322-1 (softcover)

ISBN: 978-1-4707-5323-8 (ePub)

Printed in the United States of America.

10 9 8 7 6 5 4 3 2 1   27 26 25 24 23 22 21 20 19 18

TABLE OF CONTENTS

"

So the Word
became human and
made his home among us.
He was full of unfailing love
and faithfulness. And we have
seen his glory, the glory
of the Father's one
and only Son.

"

John 1:14

INTRODUCTION

It's never been easier to get your hands on a Bible. They're handed out on street corners, given as graduation gifts, and tucked into drawers in hotel rooms. In America, almost 90 percent of households have one or more Bibles sitting on bookshelves or bedside tables.

And that's generally where they stay: unopened and unread.

Because—let's be honest—while *getting* a Bible is easy, actually *reading* it? Not so much.

For starters, the Bible is a thick brick of a book, usually running more than a thousand pages. It crisscrosses cultures and centuries, ricochets between nomadic tribes, royal courts, and the occasional harem.

Plus, it's a mishmash of poetry, prophecy, personal letters, songs, statutes, history, and hair-raising apocalyptic warnings. There are about a zillion names you can't pronounce and places Google Maps has never heard of.

It's tough sorting out how all the parts and pieces fit together. Where to start. What passages mean. Even what translation to use.

No wonder wading into the Bible can be overwhelming.

Until now.

Because reading the Bible is about to get a *lot* easier with this little book.

We'll help you get started in the Bible and answer some of the Big Questions about the Bible. We'll even keep things interesting by suggesting a few Bible-related experiments to try.

Relax. The experiments are just that: *experiments*.

If they work, you'll experience the Bible in new, dynamic ways. You'll be less baffled and more at home in the Bible.

And even better: You'll not only read the book, but you'll also meet its Author.

If an experiment doesn't work, just move on to the next one—you'll eventually find something that helps you better connect with the Bible.

We promise.

But *you* make a promise to *us*, too: Promise to give these experiments a try.

Promise?

Good. Then let's get started.

Whether you're a first-time Bible reader or an experienced, through-the-Bible-in-a-year veteran, we're glad you're here.

Let's pull out a Bible and—believe it or not—have some fun!

" I tell
you the truth,
until heaven and
earth disappear,
not even the smallest
detail of God's law
will disappear until
its purpose is
achieved. "

Matthew 5:18

HELP! HOW DO I READ THE BIBLE... AND WHY BOTHER AT ALL?

Why bother reading the Bible when there are so many quicker ways to find out what's in it?

Plenty of smart people who study the Bible are lined up to give you the inside scoop. So why not just fire up their podcasts, sit through their sermons, or read their blogs and call it good? Why go to the trouble of reading the Bible yourself?

Because if you don't, you're missing the entire point.

God didn't give you the Bible so you could master the material in it. When you stand in front of God in heaven, you won't be there because you aced a 10-question quiz about the details in his book.

What will matter most then—and matters most now—is your friendship with God.

And *that's* the purpose of the Bible—to help you discover the heart of God, to become familiar with the pulse of his love. As you see what and who God values, as you hear his words speaking through the Bible, you get an ever-better sense of who he is.

And that seldom happens when you rely on others to filter God's voice and explain him to you.

Is there value in listening to what the experts say about the Bible? Sure—and we'll get into that later. But don't settle for mining the Bible for *information* when you could be experiencing *transformation.*

The single most important decision you can make about reading the Bible is to read it—not to study it—to draw closer to God.

It's all about relationship.

And that relationship is best seen in the person of Jesus.

He's what God's love looks like when it shows up wearing skin.

He's at the very center of not just God's heart, but the Bible itself. If you're meeting Jesus as you read the Bible, you're on solid ground—even if you're not an expert.

For some reason, people love studying the Bible, poking into every nook and cranny, digging for one more detail. While that's not necessarily a bad thing, it can be a distraction. Knowing details about the Bible doesn't amount to much if you miss the bigger picture.

Consider what might be the most spectacular Bible study ever—one that happened on a dusty road between Jerusalem and the town of Emmaus.

Two men are walking, Jerusalem slowly disappearing behind them as they make their way home.

They're tired and discouraged, and their hunched shoulders show it. So does their conversation, which is all about Jesus.

Jesus, the rabbi they'd heard speak and decided to follow.

Jesus, who had healed lepers, fed thousands with just a handful of fish and crusts of bread, and raised the dead.

They'd believed in Jesus, and then the unthinkable happened.

An arrest. A cross. A tomb.

And now they're walking home, trailing a cloud of dust and disappointment behind them.

They hardly notice when another man falls in step beside them. A stranger who listens for a few moments and then asks them to explain what's happened. Who is this Jesus they keep talking about?

They tell the stranger everything—about what Jesus has done and how their hopes died with him, how their dreams for a new kingdom lay buried with the rabbi.

The stranger hears them and then does something amazing: He connects the dots between Scriptures both men *know* but have never fully *understood.* He walks them through familiar passages, helping them see how nothing that's happened is a mistake, how it's all been planned for centuries. And how this Jesus they loved and lost is at the center of it all.

They feel as if they've been blind. They know all those passages from the Law and Prophets—every Jewish boy knows them by heart. But they've never really understood them until this moment.

So of course they invite the stranger to dinner. Not just because it's polite but because there's something about him. Something…well, they can't quite say.

Until he prays and cracks open a loaf of bread.

And *then* they know.

And Jesus disappears.

These two men who dragged their feet the seven miles from Jerusalem to Emmaus, staggering under the weight of fear and disappointment, almost fly as they dash back to Jerusalem to share the news.

They've seen Jesus! He's alive! And his words, even before they fully understood who he was, burn in their hearts. They at last could see past the details to the big picture. They had the full story.

And it came not because they pried one more fact out of Scripture, but because of a relationship. Jesus breathed fresh life into passages the men already knew as he revealed himself through those familiar words. If you want to read the story yourself, check out Luke 24:13-53.

To be sure, the Bible isn't the *only* way Jesus may make himself known to you. He has plenty of tricks up his sleeve, and there's no putting him in a box.

But the Bible is one way, and that's why it's a poor decision to outsource spending time in the Bible to others. You give up the opportunity for Jesus to engage you there—and that's a missed opportunity indeed.

So why bother to read the Bible?

Because you're looking for more than data points— you're looking to meet a friend there.

The Bible is the living, breathing Word of God, still every bit as powerful as when Jesus spoke to the men on that road to Emmaus. And equally able to burn in your heart the way Jesus' words burned in theirs.

As you pursue the heart of God and the person of Jesus, expect the Bible to take on new meaning. To speak to you as it's not spoken before.

It's worth listening because the voice you hear is none other than the voice of God.

By the way, turn to page 155 if you'd like to see how well you'd do on that quiz God won't be giving you. We scored 4 out of 10—and we wrote the quiz.

Maybe you can do better.

PAUSE TO PONDER

People come to the Bible for lots of reasons.

Some because they're at a crossroads and want guidance. Should they take the new job offer? sign that contract? say yes to the marriage proposal?

Others come looking for rules to live by—for the security of knowing the right thing to do in every situation.

And then there are those who just don't want to feel guilty. They flip through a Bible now and then because that's what good Christians do, right?

What about you? Why are you coming to the Bible?

As clearly as you can, and in just a few lines, explain your motivation:

The Bible has the potential to deepen and energize our relationship with Jesus, not just our knowledge of him. How has reading the Bible in the past helped or hurt your relationship with Jesus?

EXPERIMENT 1: Getting Ready

For this experiment you'll need a sticky note or another easy-to-use bookmark. Rustle one up now, please.

We can wait…

You back?

Now turn to the Table of Contents in your Bible and mark the page so it's easy to find in the future.

We'll be asking you to turn to specific passages in your Bible, and it will be a lot easier if you use the Table of Contents to find them. Perhaps you have friends who can instantly find any Bible passage because they've memorized the order of the books, but if that's not you, it's not a problem.

Remember: The goal isn't to master the *mechanics* of the Bible. The goal is to experience the *message* of the Bible. To pursue the heart of God and let him more fully transform you into the person he's created you to be.

While the Table of Contents isn't technically an inspired portion of the Bible, we're lobbying for it to get an upgrade. Anything that helpful is definitely a gift from God.

HELP! HOW DO I READ THE BIBLE... WHEN I DON'T KNOW WHICH VERSION TO USE?

For Dave, it was easier to pick out a car than a Bible.

He decided to replace the Bible he'd been given as a child, so Dave visited a Christian bookstore. His mission: Buy a Bible.

"I asked the clerk to show me what they had," Dave remembers. "She walked me to the back of the store and pointed to a wall. It was filled—floor to ceiling—with shelves full of Bibles. I had no idea where to start."

The clerk asked Dave what translation he wanted, but Dave had assumed there were just two: King James and Other. He had no idea what the flurry of initials she tossed around meant. NLT? NLV? NASB? He was drowning in alphabet soup.

So she tried narrowing Dave's choices with a series of questions.

Did he want a study Bible? a reference Bible? maybe a parallel Bible?

What sort of cover did he prefer—hard, soft, leather, leatherette? What color?

Any thoughts about devotional content? Was he, by chance, dealing with divorce, addiction, parenting or marriage issues, or a challenging job?

"I finally told her to bring me whatever Bible she thought was best," Dave says.

The clerk paused, plucked a Bible off a shelf, and asked Dave to begin reading in Matthew, chapter 6.

"She asked me to notice if anything got between me and taking in what Jesus said and did. If the language was too confusing, or the print too small, she'd recommend an alternative. If text tucked in the margins was distracting, she had Bibles without that, too."

Over the course of the next 20 minutes, Dave zeroed in on the Bible he still has today: A hardcover New Living Translation that's so worn some of the pages have worked loose.

"I'd replace it with another copy, but this one's an old friend," Dave admits. "I'd rather give my dog up for adoption."

The clerk who helped Dave pick a Bible had nailed it: The best translation for Dave was whatever one best helped him focus on Jesus. All the bells and whistles in the world ("Ostrich-leather cover! Built-in pockets! Full Greek-English Dictionary!") didn't matter if Dave's new Bible failed to help him know, love, and befriend Jesus.

And she was right about something else: Not all Bibles are created equal. Different translations have different strengths, and picking the right one will help you enjoy reading it.

So you know: There's no perfect translation of the Bible. The various books included in the Bible were originally written in Hebrew, Greek, and Aramaic, and scholars don't always agree exactly how passages should be translated. Plus, figures of speech tossed into the text seldom translate well.

For instance, when future generations unearth a time capsule buried in the 1960s, they'll struggle to understand the precise meaning of "Far out! Groovy, man!" (Not that anyone was quite sure what it meant in the '60s, either.)

Some versions of the Bible aim to be literal translations from the original languages. Other versions give translators room to interpret what they believe original texts intended to say, using more of a thought-for-thought approach.

Either way, don't hold out for the perfect translation. It's not out there.

But you *will* find a translation or two that fit you well, that help you grow in your friendship with God. That help you best see the heart of God lived out in the person of Jesus.

With that in mind, here's a quick list of five common translations—and our take on the strengths of each.

• The **King James Version** is poetic and memorable and uses words you won't find anywhere outside of 17th-century England. It can be tough to understand but remains a bestseller.

• The **English Standard Version** gets as close as possible to the wording of the earliest known texts. If you value a literal translation, this might be the one for you. Just know it's also not the easiest read.

• The **New Living Translation** is not only literal, but also highly readable. This is where Dave landed, and we admit it: We like it, too.

• The **New International Version** walks the line between a word-for-word translation and a thought-for-thought approach. And it does a great job. It's definitely worth a look.

• ***The Message*** was written by Eugene Peterson, who translated from Greek and Hebrew into modern English, paraphrasing as he went. It counts among its fans many people who've read the Bible often, so they appreciate Peterson's fresh wording of familiar passages.

Which version of the Bible is best for you is your call—but review these five and any others your Bible-reading friends say they like. Don't assume the Bible handed to you when you were a child or handed down from Great-Grandma Edna is the best choice for you now.

By the way, consider using a Bible that's not over-cluttered with lots of sidebars and footnotes.

While they can be helpful, they're dangerous, too. They send a signal that the Bible is a reference book, and the goal is to dissect passages and understand every nuance and shade of meaning.

When you come to the Bible seeking information rather than transformation, you lose. You miss out on seeing the big picture of God's heart as he works in and through his creation.

Especially if you're just getting started in the Bible, pick up the simplest, cleanest version you can find of your favorite translation—just the Bible text. That way you can read it without voices whispering in your ear about details that are far less important than letting God speak to you through the Bible itself.

Though, if you're going to use a Bible with additional content in the margins, we have a suggestion: Use the *Jesus-Centered Bible.* It's a New Living Translation, and it highlights how Jesus is present throughout the Bible, including in the books of the Old Testament.

That's helpful to know—and it helps keep your focus where it needs to be.

Some readers go all the way and look for versions of the Bible that don't even include chapter and verse numbers. Those weren't part of the original manuscripts and tend to encourage paying attention to snippets rather than the larger themes of a passage.

See page 26 for an example of how verse numbers and commentary can sometimes be distractions.

The bottom line: The Bible is powerful and alive—the very Word of God. It's one place God can meet you, deepening your friendship with him. Being in any version of the Bible is better than not being in one at all.

But having the right version is like having the right bike or the right hiking shoes. You feel better as you move forward and find your rhythm more quickly.

Plus, fewer blisters.

PAUSE TO PONDER

Maybe you own one copy of the Bible or you have a stack of them. Whatever your current go-to Bible is, check inside the front cover to find out what translation it is.

Then ask yourself: Is this the best version for me?

Given who you are and how you read, if you were picking out a Bible for yourself today, is this the one? If so, why? If not, why not?

Jot your thoughts below:

" It ain't those parts of the Bible that I can't understand that bother me, it is the parts that I do understand. "

—*Mark Twain*

Now, if you're willing to take a risk, ask Jesus what *he* thinks. What does he recommend: stick with what you've got or replace it?

EXPERIMENT 1: Compare and Contrast

Do what Dave did: Check out how different translations handle the same passage. And you don't even need to go to a bookstore to do it.

Assuming that Bible Gateway (BibleGateway.com) is still up and running, visit the website and read Matthew, chapter 6, in the five translations we described. Check out any others your friends recommend, too.

Which feels most natural and conversational to you? Which do you enjoy reading most?

That's the version for you as you dive into the Bible more deeply. It may not be the translation you use forever, but it's a great one for now.

By the way, there are over 150 different Bible translations at the website, so if you decide to look at them all, pack a lunch. You'll be there awhile.

If certain Bible designers (you know who you are) got their hands on a text, even a letter home, it might end up looking like this:

[1]Dear Mom,[a]

It's beautiful here in Wisconsin[b] but a long way from home.[c] Dan likes his new job, and his boss is nice. [2]The kids' school is just a 10-minute walk from the apartment. I haven't found a job yet, but something will turn up. [3]Soon, I hope! Wish you were closer—I miss you![d]

Talk soon,
Sheila

---

[a]Use of the salutation "Mom," a less formal version of "Mother," implies familiarity and presumed intimacy. [b]Located in the north-central United States, Wisconsin is best known for snowfall, pleasant residents, and cheese curds, though not necessarily in that order. [c]Two opposing attributes of Wisconsin frame the author's dilemma: a transcendent beauty that pulls her away from the essence of the familiar. See "Michigan: Winter Wonderland" in Ellis' excellent *Seasonal Splendor, Existential Angst*, Spurious Publishing, 2004, 18-27. [d]Note the relationship between circumstance and emotional satisfaction. The question arises: Does situation dictate emotion, or is the inverse true? What is the correlation between perceived reality and emotional stasis?

You get the idea.

HELP! HOW DO I READ THE BIBLE... WHEN I DON'T KNOW WHERE TO START?

Think of the Bible as a swimming pool: There's a deep end and a shallow end.

If you're just getting started with the Bible, you'll want to be in the shallow end. Save the high dive for later.

It's tempting to pick up the Bible and read it like every other book you've held: Flip to the first page and start reading, which actually gets you to some interesting stuff.

You're in Genesis, where you'll see the power and majesty of God up close. You'll discover the Bible's account of Creation and see how life looks without sin in it. There's adventure and intrigue, and for the most part, the book of Genesis is a page-turner. You'll probably zip straight through it in just a few sittings.

Exodus keeps up the pace, carrying you through the history of the Jewish people and their interactions with God.

But then the Bible slams on the brakes with the book of Leviticus.

It's a quagmire of religious rules, procedures for burnt offerings, blood offerings, and general mayhem regarding farm animals. It reads like a manual for keeping God happy because, well, that's pretty much what it is…though it's a system for relating to God that Jesus has turned on its head.

Assuming you make it through 27 chapters about how to slaughter animal sacrifices, you'll then run into the book of Numbers, which leads off with a census report.

And that's probably where you'll stop reading.

So let's not do that.

Yes, the Old Testament is valuable, but it's not the best place to start your Bible-reading career. Opinions vary, but we'd like to recommend you jump into the Bible with the book of Mark.

Don't know where that is? Check the Table of Contents—it's the second book in the New Testament.

The book of Mark shows you what Jesus did while on earth, giving you a ringside seat for his three-year ministry. You'll see how he treated people and how he lived out his mission of bringing forgiveness to those who were willing to trust him.

Finished with Mark? Skip past the book of Luke and read the book of John.

John, one of Jesus' closest friends, will tell you what Jesus said. There's plenty of overlap between Mark and John, and that's a good thing. You'll deepen your understanding of who Jesus is and what he has to say to you.

Then keep going to the book of Acts. It's the Apostle Luke's description of how the early church was launched as Jesus' followers spread the message of God's love.

From there you're ready for the book of Romans, the Apostle Paul's summary of the basic teachings of the Christian faith.

Then backtrack to the book of Luke. What little we know about Jesus' early life we learn here, and when you read knowing what's coming, it's inspiring.

Maybe you noticed: As you've read through Mark, John, Acts, Romans, and Luke, you've waded into deeper water. You have a solid understanding of who

Jesus is and what he thinks of you. And you've formed your opinion of him—perhaps deciding he's someone you want to know better.

So pull off the water wings—it's time to dog paddle into the deep end of the pool.

Read through the psalms—not all at once; there are 150 of them—and see how often David and the other writers sum up what you're feeling, too. See how boldly they come to God, how transparently honest they are.

That's the sort of friendship God wants with you, too. One in which you tell him how you're really feeling, what you really think. You, too, can come to him in times of trouble and laugh with him when he delights you.

Read Genesis and Exodus, looking for how Jesus has always been part of the story, how he's at the very center of the Bible. Using the *Jesus-Centered Bible* will be a huge help, but be aware—you may see something other than what the writers and editors of that Bible saw. God may show you things they didn't see, and that's okay.

Take your time as you read. It's okay—more than okay—to pause often and ask God to reveal himself.

Ask questions, lots of them.

But rather than ask *what's* happening, ask *why* it's happening…and what it reveals. As you see God act, what's he unveiling about himself? about you? Talk with him about your insights and see what else he has to say.

And now that you're doing swan dives with the best of them, make your way to Isaiah and some of the other prophets. The truths God had for his people back in the day are the same truths he has for you. And how those truths were received (or not) by those people…well, that may feel familiar, too.

Then one day, fortified by a good breakfast and a multi-vitamin or two, dutifully trudge through the book of Leviticus.

This is what you've been freed from. *This* is what the loving sacrifice of Jesus—which you've read about again and again—completed once and for all. *This* is what your friendship with God has unshackled you from.

Read and be grateful.

Read and be free.

PAUSE TO PONDER

If you're someone who enjoys reading, consider: What *sort* of things do you enjoy reading?

Are you a history buff?

A fan of how-to writing?

Enjoy poetry?

Like a good romance?

You can find all of that in the Bible, so to keep things interesting, seek out sections that naturally appeal to you. There's really no wrong place to jump into the Bible, but there are definitely spots that are more or less relevant to you.

Here are some suggestions for which sections of the Bible fit different literary genres. Keep an eye out for Jesus in all of these portions of the Bible—he's there.

Adventure—Genesis, Exodus, Acts...the Bible's packed with adventure. Strap in when you're reading; things move fast.

Poetry—Psalms, of course, but there's beautiful imagery throughout the Bible. Check out the book of Ecclesiastes, too.

How To—You'll find great advice for building a rewarding life in Proverbs. And read what Jesus has to say in Matthew, chapters 5 and 6.

Romance—The Song of Solomon. It's sexy and steamy—no wonder it hardly ever gets picked for sermons.

History—The book of Exodus has your name all over it. This book tells the grand story of God rescuing his people from slavery while also pulling back the curtain on the personal lives of key leaders.

Biography—Head for the Gospels—Matthew, Mark, Luke, and John. That's where you'll get the most direct view of Jesus. The book of Acts does a good job describing the Apostle Paul, too—and not always in a sympathetic way.

Humor—Back to the Gospels again. Jesus' parables and teachings have been so thoroughly studied that the humor has been wrung out of them, but much of what Jesus said must have caused his original audiences to guffaw. The camel trying to get through the eye of a needle, for instance, is classic.

Mystery—The book of Revelation holds enough mystery to keep you busy for a long while.

A question: If you were being guided just by the type of literature you enjoy reading, where would you start in the Bible?

Now give it a try.

EXPERIMENT 1: Adventures in Reading

How comfortable are you with the idea that God might use the same Bible passage to say one thing to you and something else to your neighbor?

Some people find comfort in thinking that every verse in the Bible can be interpreted just one way.

That makes reading the Bible safe, simple, and predictable. Three words, by the way, you'll never be able to apply to Jesus.

Try this: Turn in your Bible to John 8:1-11. It's an account of Jesus being set up by some religious leaders to condemn a woman who'd been caught in the act of adultery.

Before you start reading, ask God to show you something in the passage you've not seen before—assuming you've read it before.

Don't settle for just rehashing what others—all those devotions and sermons and commentary entries—have told you about this passage. Be open to hearing from God, and hearing something fresh.

Consider this an adventure.

Once you've finished reading, jot what God shows you below:

EXPERIMENT 2: Asking the Better Question

That tendency to treat the Bible like a homework assignment is hard to shake. If you're like most people, you've been conditioned to process what you read in the Bible through your head while your heart hangs around, lounging against the wall and sighing.

You read and then ask what just happened. You want to get the facts straight.

Wanting to understand what you read isn't a bad thing. But if that's where you stop, you miss out on relationship. You leave a lot on the table that your friend God means for you to carry away with you.

Do this: Read John 8:1-11 again. When you're finished, jot your answers to two questions:

What did Jesus do?

Why do you think Jesus did what he did?

_____

_____

_____

_____

_____

_____

We're guessing that second question pulled you more deeply into the passage. It prompted you to be more than just an observer; it opened you to Jesus.

When you read the Bible, ask far more *why* questions than *what* questions.

Jesus is waiting for you in the why far more often than in the what.

JUST
CURIOUS:

WHERE DID THE BIBLE COME FROM?

Great question.

Here's a two-minute answer:

The book we call the Bible is actually a collection of 66 separate books written over a span of some 1,600 years. The authors—about 40 of them—range from kings to fishermen, with an especially well-educated tent-maker named Paul accounting for a sizable chunk of the New Testament.

The books of the Old Testament (the Jewish Scriptures) started as oral accounts—history repeated from generation to generation. Eventually that history was written down, and by the time Jesus was born, those Hebrew books had been translated into Greek.

It's that Greek translation (the Septuagint) that early Christians had in mind when they referred to Scripture.

Creating the New Testament books took far less time—several hundred years.

But it took an additional century for early church leaders to decide which books should be considered holy, treated with the same respect given to the Jewish Scriptures.

In A.D. 367, the bishop of Alexandria identified 27 books he felt were authoritative and worthy. The New Testament now comprises those same books.

Still, not everyone agreed with that 66-book list for the Old and New Testaments. That's why some Bibles still include extra books (the Apocrypha), books that didn't quite make the cut. These Bibles are most often associated with the Roman Catholic and Greek and Russian Orthodox Christian traditions.

In the fifth century, the Bible was translated into Latin, which at that time was the international language of scholarship. That version, called the Vulgate, became the Bible's standard text for the next thousand years, well into the Middle Ages.

But then the printing press arrived and, with it, the ability to make the Bible available to an increasingly literate world. Bible translators—Martin Luther and

William Tyndale among them—trumpeted the value of individual believers having the opportunity to read the Bible for themselves.

The floodgates opened, and now there are literally hundreds of Bible translations in a wide range of languages.

There. A two-minute explanation, in case you were wondering.

And something else, in case you were wondering: None of this will be on an exam.

"

The grass
withers and the
flowers fade,
but the word
of our God
stands forever.

"

Isaiah 40:8

HELP! HOW DO I READ THE BIBLE... WHEN THE BIBLE'S SO INTIMIDATING?

We get it. If the Bible is a holy book, it's a little intimidating to go poking around in. It feels safer to respect the Bible from a distance.

Unfortunately, that's how many people have been raised to respond to the Bible.

In some churches, everyone stands when the Bible is read aloud, treating it the way you'd treat visiting royalty. The Bible sits on an altar—alone, elevated, and illuminated.

It's made perfectly clear that reading the Bible should be done soberly, after serious preparation and soul-searching.

The not-so-hidden message: You're welcome, but not worthy.

Small wonder anyone raised to see the Bible as so otherworldly on Sunday mornings can't easily cozy up with it throughout the week.

Well…it's time to get over that.

The Bible never asks to be revered from a distance. It asks to move from the page into your life, finding a home in your mind and heart.

God's looking to transform you, not just soak up your reverence. As your friend, he's after what's best for you, and that's time with him…including time in the Bible.

So what's the best way for less-than-perfect people like you (okay, us, too…) to approach God's written Word?

Glad you asked.

Come With Assurance

God's not hiding from you, and the Bible isn't a coded message that requires a seminary-degree decoder ring to decipher.

God *wants* to connect with you in the Bible, so don't overthink this.

You'll never be adequately prepared to dissect every verse of the Bible, to answer every question, to write every academic footnote. Even people who translate the Bible for a living aren't—and will tell you so.

But you're *perfectly* prepared to come to the Bible to be with God. He's called you his friend and given you a standing invitation to tug at his elbow whenever you wish. To spend time with him wherever—and whenever—you want.

Including in the Bible.

When you open your Bible expecting that God will meet you there, your expectation will always be met, often far beyond anything you could anticipate.

So don't feel intimidated. Feel invited.

Come With Anticipation

Come to the Bible the same way you come to God: expecting God to speak to you. And when a passage almost jumps off the page and grabs your attention, have a conversation with God about what just happened.

What's God wanting you to discover about him in that passage? about yourself?

It's okay if you plan to read three chapters, and in the first few verses, God zings you with a truth that stops you in your tracks. Just close your Bible and talk with him about it. That's what friends do: They adjust their plans to be fully present to each other, to listen and respond to each other.

Come With Humility

Hard to believe, but this Bible-reading thing isn't all about you.

God uses the Bible to do lots of things. To help shape you into the person he created you to be. To inspire you to take action. Or maybe just to spend time with you because friends do that.

Come to the Bible open to all of that and anything else God might have for you. Set aside every expectation other than this: God is ready and waiting to connect with you.

See where he takes it from there.

Come Prayerfully

Reading the Bible is an extension of your ongoing conversation with God. It's as much prayer as if you were talking directly with him. Because the Bible is one place God can—and will—talk directly to you.

So be mindful of God's presence as you read. He's at your elbow, nudging you to see his heart in the pages you're turning.

Come With an Open Mind

Most people have at least a few doubts about the Bible. That's okay—we have doubts about everything else, too. The government. The justice system. All those mysterious charges your bank tosses in for ATM usage.

But do this: Leave your doubts at the door when you come to the Bible. Ask God to speak to you—perhaps about your doubts—as you read, and see what happens.

Rather than try to shape the Bible, let it shape you. Let the truth and beauty you encounter soothe you even if you're unsure how everything in the Bible works. Even if you're not all that certain God is always with you.

God is keeping an open mind about you. Do the same about him.

Come With a Sense of Humor

Friends have fun together—and there are times reading the Bible is just a hoot.

You've just had a knock-down, drag-out fight with a friend or spouse because you were somehow offended—and you find yourself reading a passage about humility.

You're bored and yawning, and there's Paul sharing his faith and turning the world upside down.

You're feeling overwhelmed at work and somehow make your way to the passage about Elijah facing hundreds of hostile false prophets on a mountaintop, prophets who'd like nothing more than to rip his head off when Elijah is just doing his job.

Sometimes God can't help himself; he leads you to self-discovery with a biblical pie in the face.

Roll with it—your Friend is playing with you.

Come Ready to Do Something

When Brent handed his buddy a Bible, Brent was taking a risk.

"Dan was dragged to church as a child, and now that he was 30, he was done with all that," Brent says. "But we'd had a few faith-based conversations, and I felt it was time to give him a Bible. I told him to read the Gospels and then we'd talk about his concerns."

A few nights later Brent was startled by insistent knocking at his front door.

There stood Dan, Bible in hand.

"Dan told me he was frustrated as he read through the Gospels because there was no way he could do everything Jesus asked of his followers," says Brent. "So he decided to keep reading, and when he got to Acts, there it was: something he *could* do. He could be like those people who heard Peter at Pentecost: He could admit he believed and be baptized.

"Dan knew I had a bathtub, and he wanted to be baptized. Right away. So we did it. And when Dan read through the Gospels again, he did it with a fresh understanding: He wasn't alone. As he joined with Jesus, God himself fueled a steady transformation in Dan."

That may be your experience as you read the Bible, too. You may read a passage and know God's giving you something to do. Right away. Now.

If—*when*—that happens, know you're not going to do it alone.

Your Friend is with you.

PAUSE TO PONDER

What has shaped how you approach the Bible?

Perhaps you were raised in a church or home that treated the Bible like a holy relic, something to be admired but not touched.

Maybe you were forced to read the Bible as a child or never even saw a Bible until just recently.

Whatever has shaped your view of the Bible, describe it here with words or drawings:

_____

_____

_____

_____

_____

Now talk with Jesus about what you've written or drawn.

What does he have to say about how you've viewed the Bible in the past...and now?

EXPERIMENT 1: Random Reading

Find a comfortable place and settle in with a Bible.

Open the Bible at random and read a chapter. Really. Just plop it open anywhere.

When you've finished reading, jot down your responses to these two questions:

• What did God reveal about himself and his heart in this chapter?

• And what does this chapter and your response to it reveal about you?

EXPERIMENT 2: Humility Practice

If you're like most of us, humility isn't your default setting. But if humility helps with Bible reading, then get some humility practice today as you…

• Try to understand other points of view. Accepting what's said to you doesn't mean you endorse it. So graciously welcome the opinions of others today.

• Aim to be teachable. What can you learn from people you meet today, including that guy who cut you off in traffic?

• Give your critical streak a rest. Simply enjoy others today without feeling the need to correct or give advice.

• Embrace being open to change. Maybe your way isn't the only way after all. How might you think and behave in new ways? What difference might those changes bring to your life?

After a day spent practicing humility (it's gonna be tiring...), talk with God about this: How might you bring that same humility to reading the Bible?

EXPERIMENT 3: Deal With Your Doubts

Doubts aren't bad in themselves—it depends on what you do with them. They can actually be huge opportunities for growth, but only if you'll own and articulate them.

So do this: Write down any doubts you have concerning the Bible. Be honest; nobody's looking over your shoulder.

Now call a friend and tell that person what you wrote.

Be clear that you aren't asking for answers—you're calling so you can talk openly about doubts that have been rattling around in your head. Explain that you're interested in getting them out on the table so you can see them more clearly.

After you have that conversation, have another one. This time, with God.

Ask Jesus to meet you anywhere you're experiencing doubt, just as he did with those two friends on the road to Emmaus. And ask him to help you hear him in every way he wants to speak to you—including through the Bible.

"

The instructions of the Lord
are perfect, reviving the soul.
The decrees of the Lord are trustworthy,
making wise the simple. The commandments
of the Lord are right, bringing joy to the
heart. The commands of the Lord are clear,
giving insight for living. Reverence for the
Lord is pure, lasting forever. The laws of
the Lord are true; each one is fair. They are
more desirable than gold, even the finest
gold. They are sweeter than honey, even
honey dripping from the comb. They are a
warning to your servant, a great reward
for those who obey them.

"

Psalm 19:7-11

HELP! HOW DO I READ THE BIBLE...
WHEN I'M AFRAID I'LL GET IT WRONG?

If you're taking time to read the Bible, it makes sense for you to want to understand what you're reading. And just as much sense for you not to want to *misunderstand* it, to wander off into the weeds. To pull the wrong lessons out of Jesus' parables or assume that something Paul wrote is a hard-and-fast rule for all Christians in all places at all times when it's really just a cultural reference.

But short of mastering a couple of ancient languages and picking up a theology Ph.D. in your spare time, how can you be sure you're staying on track? How can you feel confident the Bible says what you think it says?

Well…you can't. Not completely. There are a few spots in the Bible—just a few—that even the experts can't sort out with 100-percent certainty.

So know you're in good company. To some extent everyone who picks up a Bible shares your concern—even Professor Smarty Pants who makes a living lecturing about this stuff.

But if you'll do as the good professor does and keep in mind a few simple truths about approaching the Bible, you can rest assured you're interpreting what you read with a great deal of accuracy.

In the world of seminaries, this is called hermeneutics—the science and art of biblical interpretation.

In our world we call it Eight Things to Do Right. And here they are…

1. Remember Why You've Come

You're reading for relationship, so be open at any time for God to interrupt you and ask you to pay extra attention to something you've just read. Often it will be a passage that speaks to you about a concern in your life that's only loosely connected to the text in front of you.

When the author of 1 John wrote about "a craving for physical pleasure" (1 John 2:16), it's safe to assume he didn't have internet porn in mind. But that's what Greg thought of when he read those words.

"It's not like I was a porn addict," he says. "I could go long stretches without pulling up a website. But it was a real thing in my life, and it was taking a toll on my marriage."

Greg believes God used what he read in 1 John to bring conviction into his life, to highlight an area where change was needed.

That change was for Greg to rely more fully on his friendship with God and to build boundaries in his life that rekindled his relationship with his wife.

Was any of that in the text? No, but God used the text to give Greg fresh insight and to prompt significant change because Greg was reading not just for intellectual understanding but also with an eye on his friendship with God.

Which leads to the second thing to keep in mind...

2. Prayerfully Invite the Holy Spirit to Guide You

When Jesus said the Holy Spirit's work includes guiding Jesus' followers into truth (John 16:13), Jesus didn't point to a Bible. But it's not a stretch to assume that part of that truth-guiding involves helping

Christians who read the Bible to meet Jesus there, to discover truth in the words of Scripture.

So when you read the Bible, be aware there's more happening than when you're reading the latest issue of your favorite magazine. There's a spiritual dynamic at play, one you can encourage by honestly, prayerfully inviting the Holy Spirit to show you what God wants you to see in the passage you're reading.

3. Keep in Mind the Literary Context

Because the Bible contains lots of types of literature—poetry and history among them—be mindful of the type of passage you're reading.

If you're reading poetry, expect lots of word pictures that were never intended to be taken literally. Solomon describes his soul mate's breasts as twin gazelles grazing among the lilies (Song of Solomon 4:5). If that's literal, someone besides the lilies has a problem.

But if you're reading in the book of Acts, which describes what real people did in real places, the text is far likelier to be intended to be taken at face value.

Though, even in historical books such as the book of Matthew, make allowances for figures of speech. When Jesus describes false prophets coming disguised as sheep when they're really wolves (Matthew 7:15), his audience then and now gets his point without imagining guys wearing sheep costumes.

4. Remember There's a Historical Context

Here's where a Bible commentary can be of significant help—more about those later.

Because the books of the Bible were originally introduced to specific cultures in specific times, the text is loaded with cultural references. Phrases and examples all had a significance that can be lost when you don't know the cultural, military, and political context.

For example, consider what Jesus says in Matthew 5:41: "If a soldier demands that you carry his gear for a mile, carry it two miles."

It's hard for contemporary readers to get the full impact of that statement because they may not know that the soldiers Jesus referred to were *enemy* soldiers. They were Roman troops, part of an occupying force in Israel during Jesus' time.

So this isn't about doing a favor for some friendly, footsore soldier who serves on the home team. It's an enemy soldier demanding a civilian go a mile out of his way while hauling a heavy backpack. And with nothing by way of thanks at the end of the trip but a swift kick.

Adds a new dimension to Jesus' statement, doesn't it?

Those "oh, *now* I get it" light bulbs pop on all the time in the Bible once you have a bit of historical background. So if you don't quite understand a passage, check the historical context. Getting that in focus often clears up a question.

A practice related to context is sometimes called proof texting—yanking a verse or two out of context to make a point or stake a claim on a promise made by God. It's a common practice and can lead to unfortunate results.

For instance, Jesus told his closest followers they could drink poison and handle poisonous snakes without ill consequence. It's a promise that was later tested by Paul when the shipwrecked apostle was bitten by a deadly viper (Acts 28:3-6).

But does that promise Jesus made extend to all believers in all times? Some have claimed the answer is yes and have suffered for getting hold of the wrong end of a rattler.

A similar outcome is likely for those who read Jesus' invitation to step out of a boat and walk on water. Others can step…but they'd best know how to swim.

To see how far afield ignoring context can lead you, check out "The Problem With Proof Texting" on page 151.

Then go and sin no more, especially if you create out-of-context Scripture memes for social media.

5. Identify the Original Audience and Author

Here's another way a commentary can be useful.

Sometimes books of the Bible actually tell you who was initially on the receiving end of a letter from Paul or a prophecy from Isaiah. But just having a name doesn't tell you much about *why* the book was written and why the writer thought it important to send it to a specific person or group.

For instance, Paul's letter to the church in Galatia (the book of Galatians) makes a lot more sense when you understand that the early church was composed of Jewish converts who thought following Jewish traditions was a prerequisite for being a Christ-follower.

The members of that church were Gentiles (non-Jews) who were under pressure from Jewish converts to not only embrace Jesus, but also to embrace Jewish customs.

Customs like…circumcision.

Which was *definitely* something Paul hadn't mentioned when he led the men in Galatia to Jesus and into the church. You can imagine their enthusiasm when they heard about that little detail after the fact.

Paul's letter is all about straightening up the misperception that the road to Jesus is through Jewish customs. That insight clears up why Paul seemed so obsessed about circumcision.

Other Bible books have similar stories. Knowing who wrote them and why they were written sheds a great deal of light on what you read. And with Bible commentaries readily available online and in your closest Christian bookstore, this is easy-to-find information.

6. Keep It Simple

Almost always, the simplest, most obvious meaning of a passage is the right one. Neither the Bible writers nor the God who inspired them was out to layer hidden meanings in the Bible. The intent was to be understood.

So when someone shows up promoting a formula, algorithm, or some other system that claims to mystically reveal the *real* meaning of the Bible, just say no thanks.

Even without the benefit of a stack of commentaries, you can easily grasp the meaning of Bible passages. Add to that your desire to understand what you're reading and the coaching of the Holy Spirit, and you're in great shape.

7. Use the Bible to Interpret the Bible

Sometimes a particular Bible passage is a bit muddy. Maybe it's the translator's fault; maybe there was a mustard stain on the original manuscript—who knows?—but you struggle to decipher the meaning.

So do this: Take a look at what's said and see if the topic is addressed in a more straightforward fashion elsewhere in the Bible.

If it's true that Jesus doesn't contradict himself, if he's the same yesterday, today, and forever (Hebrews 13:8), then applying what you learn in the straightforward passage should shed light on the less clear passage.

Another tip: Use the New Testament to help understand the Old Testament. God has revealed more about himself over time, especially through Jesus. You have the benefit of seeing how that ongoing revelation has played out.

8. Stay Centered on Jesus

No matter what Bible passage you're reading, it can teach you about the heart of God: who he is, what he intends, and how he treats his friends.

And that's never more true than when you're keeping your eyes open for Jesus.

Jesus can be seen throughout the Bible, making himself known from the first glimmer of Creation to the Bible's last peek into the throne room of God described in the book of Revelation.

When you read with Jesus in mind, you're reading for relationship.

PAUSE TO PONDER

Jesus told his followers this about the Holy Spirit: "When the Spirit of truth comes, he will guide you into all truth. He will not speak on his own but will tell you what he has heard" (John 16:13).

Sounds like a perfect Bible-reading partner, right?

But be honest: How often have you invited the Holy Spirit to look over your shoulder as you've read the Bible? And, if you have done that, how much latitude have you given the Spirit to guide you into truth, to help set your reading pace and program?

Those are worthy questions because, if you had the Holy Spirit's job description in your hand, you'd see it's essentially this: *The Spirit will lead you closer to God through Jesus.*

And isn't that why you're reading the Bible in the first place?

Talk with Jesus about this: Where do you want to take me? And how can I be more open to the Holy Spirit's leading as we take that journey together?

Jot what you hear from him below. Any nudge… visual image…snippet of a Bible verse—anything at all. Write or draw it, and then consider what Jesus is telling you.

> **"**
> There have been
> prophets and students who handle
> the Bible like a child's box of bricks;
> they explain to us the design and
> structure and purpose; but as time
> goes on things do not work out in
> their way at all. They have mistaken
> the scaffolding for the structure,
> while all the time God is working
> out His purpose with a great
> and undeterred patience.
> **"**
>
> —*Oswald Chambers*

DO I *REALLY* HAVE TO MEMORIZE BIBLE VERSES?

N_{o.}

See? How easy was *that*?

To be fair, those who advocate memorizing Scripture have their reasons:

First, Jesus did it. When confronted by Satan, he quoted Deuteronomy and Psalms to the devil. And Satan backed off (Matthew 4:1-11).

Second, there's a passage in the Bible (Psalm 119:11) that urges believers to hide God's Word in their hearts. Whether memorizing Bible verses is what that verse is really about is questionable, but fans of Bible memorization quote it often. And being who they are, they do it with stunning accuracy.

So it's safe to say that memorizing Bible passages won't hurt you—but it's by no means a requirement.

The religious leaders Jesus blasted for arrogance and hypocrisy could quote Scripture, but the truth of Scripture hadn't moved from their heads to their hearts. They had the rules down cold, but not the relationship. Memorizing alone didn't fix what was broken in those men.

Then there's this: If you struggle with treating the Bible as something more than a textbook, memorizing *might* hurt you because memorization can divert your focus from Jesus and onto his book. If you find yourself smug about your ability to drop Bible quotes into conversations, it might be time to back off the memorization drills for a while.

And some people simply struggle with memorizing anything—they're just not wired for it.

If that's you, you're off the hook. Quit feeling guilty or inferior about your lack of Bible knowledge. It's far better to understand God's Word than to be able to parrot it on command.

But if you *can* memorize passages and you're inclined to do so, by all means go for it. It's especially helpful to commit to memory passages that are directly related to issues that God's helping you address in life.

If you're hot-tempered, perhaps memorizing James 1:19 is a good idea. Tuck it into your memory so the Holy Spirit can quickly bring it to mind when you're next tempted to murder someone who sneaked 16 items into the 15-items-or-less line at the supermarket.

Struggling with loneliness? Here's a passage for you: Psalm 145:18.

And if an unhealthy desire to have more than you can afford is causing you discomfort, commit this passage to memory: Hebrews 13:5.

If you're a memorizer, you'll find a quick list of passages related to specific issues on pages 71-73.

You're welcome.

If you're not a memorizer but are looking for relevant passages to kick off conversations with God about challenges in your life, there's a list for you on pages 71-73. Same pages because it's the same list.

And again, you're welcome.

PAUSE TO PONDER

The word *memorize* is like the word *broccoli*.

You may love or hate it, but it's a sure thing you'll have a definite reaction.

A question for you: How easily do you memorize quotes and strings of numbers? Is that something that comes easily, or is it a struggle?

If you're unsure how to answer, here's a quick test: Do you have a physical, written list of all your computer passwords sitting next to your computer because you can't trust yourself to remember them?

Yes? You're probably not into memorizing.

No? And you can still log in? Memorizing is right up your alley.

While there's no mandate to memorize Bible passages, many Jesus followers say it's useful.

Ask God if there's a passage or two he'd like you to learn well enough to at least paraphrase well.

If he says yes and you're a memorizer, do it.

If he says yes and you're not a memorizer, give it a try anyway. It must be important, or God wouldn't ask you to do it.

EXPERIMENT 1: Musical Memories

If memorizing Bible passages matters to you, one way to help it happen is by learning praise and worship choruses. Many are Scripture put to music—and learning the lyrics means you're also learning the Scripture itself.

Of course, the songs you'll catch on Christian radio and in church services may not address the passages you'd prefer to learn.

Which means you've got something to learn from Michael.

He's a professional musician who found himself in a college religion class that required him to memorize Jesus' Sermon on the Mount. But try as he might, he just couldn't do it.

"Which struck me as odd," says Michael. "I mean, I know pretty much every lyric of every song that charted in the '60s and '70s, so why couldn't I remember the sermon?"

The reason, Michael discovered, was that he'd never *sung* the sermon. Music hadn't cemented the sermon—the lyrics—in his memory.

So when Michael's turn came to recite the sermon, he pulled out his guitar and performed the sermon—and he did it perfectly.

"Though I set it to doo-wop, and I had to announce up front that the occasional 'do-wah-diddys' weren't part of the original Greek," Michael admits.

Here's something for you to try: Pick out one of the verses on pages 71-73 and set the verse to music. Any music. Write something, adapt something, steal a melody from a favorite songwriter.

Create a song, run through it a dozen times in the shower, and see if it sticks.

But be sure that you *don't* just memorize the words. Ask God how he's revealed himself—and you—in the lyrics you learn.

EXPERIMENT 2: If the Verse Fits, Wear It

Look at pages 71-73 and ask God which of the issues mentioned there is one that's on his list of Stuff the Two of You Need to Talk More About.

For instance, perhaps you struggle with being content. You just can't manage it: One look at a neighbor's new car or a glance at how much money you'd rake in if you won the lottery sends you into a nosedive. You find yourself coveting what you don't have and jealous of people who have it.

Whatever issue God shows you is on his list, pray about it. Ask God to work in you to bring you to a healthier place.

And do your best to memorize the passage.

Consider this a test—a chance to see if the Holy Spirit brings the passage to mind when you next find yourself feeling discontented. If so, maybe for you there's real value in memorizing Bible passages that address ongoing issues in your life.

BRIEF BIBLE PASSAGES
TO TUCK INTO YOUR HEART AND MIND

If it's tough to control your anger...

"Understand this, my dear brothers and sisters: You must all be quick to listen, slow to speak, and slow to get angry" (James 1:19).

If you're feeling lonely...

"The Lord is close to all who call on him, yes, to all who call on him in truth" (Psalm 145:18).

If you're discontented...

"Don't love money; be satisfied with what you have. For God has said, 'I will never fail you. I will never abandon you'" (Hebrews 13:5).

If you want to avoid making poor choices...

"If you need wisdom, ask our generous God, and he will give it to you. He will not rebuke you for asking" (James 1:5).

If it's hard to be truthful...

"A false witness will not go unpunished, and a liar will be destroyed" (Proverbs 19:9).

If you're coping with a lack of confidence...

"For I can do everything through Christ, who gives me strength" (Philippians 4:13).

If you're struggling with trusting in God's love...

"And I am convinced that nothing can ever separate us from God's love. Neither death nor life, neither angels nor demons, neither our fears for today nor our worries about tomorrow—not even the powers of hell can separate us from God's love" (Romans 8:38).

If you're dealing with grief...

"He heals the brokenhearted and bandages their wounds" (Psalm 147:3).

If you're feeling guilty...

"But if we confess our sins to him, he is faithful and just to forgive us our sins and to cleanse us from all wickedness" (1 John 1:9).

If you're facing down fear...

"So be strong and courageous, all you who put your hope in the Lord!" (Psalm 31:24).

If you're facing temptations...

"The temptations in your life are no different from what others experience. And God is faithful. He will not allow the temptation to be more than you can stand. When you are tempted, he will show you a way out so that you can endure" (1 Corinthians 10:13).

If worry keeps you up at night...

"Don't worry about anything; instead, pray about everything. Tell God what you need, and thank him for all he has done. Then you will experience God's peace, which exceeds anything we can understand. His peace will guard your hearts and minds as you live in Christ Jesus" (Philippians 4:6-7).

If you're feeling overwhelmed…

"Give all your worries and cares to God, for he cares about you" (1 Peter 5:7).

> " The Word of God
> hidden in the heart
> is a stubborn voice
> to suppress. "
>
> —*Billy Graham*

HELP! HOW DO I READ THE BIBLE... WHEN I FIND THE BIBLE SORT OF... BORING?

When we were but wee tots, here's what our moms said when we whined that we were bored: Boredom is what's left over when there's activity but no engagement.

Actually, no—they never said that to us.

What they *actually* said was to get busy or we'd get handed a list of chores so long that it would make our heads spin. So we got busy.

But there's wisdom in the thought that, if you're bored with the Bible, it's not because the Bible is a boring book. It's because you're not fully engaged with it.

Please don't feel guilty about that.

People can get bored with anything. The next time you're at an amusement park, notice how first-time roller coaster riders literally bounce as they wait in line. But once they've survived the Jaws of Death Killer Coaster 10 or 12 times…well, now it's a yawner.

So if you find the Bible boring, decide to engage it differently. Rather than do what you've always done when reading it, try something new.

And because we're in your corner, we've got some suggestions. A dozen of them—so get ready for some experiments!

But first, something for you to think about…

PAUSE TO PONDER

There's a reason Ashley and Nicole never go on vacation together.

Ashley is a fan of what's commonly known as adventure travel. For Ashley, it's not a vacation unless she carries home an amazing story and at least one fresh scar.

Nicole is a fan of what's commonly known as room service. Nicole's idea of a vacation is to lounge by the pool, skimming a book, drifting off into an occasional, sunny-side-up nap. Her proof of a great vacation? She's wearing it: a tan.

Neither of them are right or wrong—but they *are* different. Ashley would be bored to tears on Nicole's vacation, and Nicole would be sure she'd been kidnapped on Ashley's.

The point: You're not like everybody else. God wired you to be in relationship with him, but you may be more like Ashley: You and God connect best when you're paddling furiously through white water, slamming against rocks as you catapult down a canyon. For you, sitting and reading is going to be boring no matter how you do it.

Or, if you're more like Nicole, reading is ideal. You're focused and at ease snuggling into a comfortable chair and opening a Bible, a cup of tea at your elbow.

So, a question for you to consider: Are you more of an Ashley or a Nicole? Are you wired for get-up-and-go or sit-and-ponder?

Jot your insights below, and then ask Jesus how he'd answer the question.

Compare notes.

_____

_____

_____

_____

EXPERIMENT 1: Tackle a Topic

Nothing focuses your attention quite like stubbing your toe.

You may go days—_weeks_—without giving the little toe on your right foot any thought whatsoever. But crunch it into a chair leg, and that toe instantly becomes the center of your universe.

Even if someone's telling you where to go to pick up free hundred-dollar bills, you don't care. You've got some hopping and screaming to do before you can think past your wounded little piggy.

If you're dealing with a stubbed-toe issue in your life—something that has your complete attention and you can't see past it—then let that guide your Bible reading.

Whatever the issue, see what the Bible has to say about it.

Dealing with debt? Consider what the Bible says about finances...shame...hope...security...whatever touches on what you're feeling and thinking.

Shattered relationship you'd give anything to heal? The Bible speaks at length about forgiveness...trust... renewal.

A caution, though: Don't just *study* what you find in the Bible.

Instead, come to the Bible open to *transformation*.

Listen for how Jesus is speaking into your friendship—what reassurance is he offering you? In what ways is he pushing you to grow? How is he bringing healing to your wounds?

Pay attention to God's voice. Otherwise, you're just running through an academic exercise.

And expect to require some help, by the way. "When I Don't Have All Those Nifty Study Tools" (page 129) lists tools that can help you locate the Bible passages most relevant to the issue at hand.

Read the passages—in context—but also look beyond what others have identified as relevant. Ask God to lead you to insights he has for you that others haven't already stumbled across.

So...what's a stubbed toe in your world? What's an issue that's front and center in your life?

And what does the Bible say about it?

After you've taken a look, jot your thoughts about the experience of looking…reading…and responding faithfully to what you found.

What did you like and not like about this experiment? Is there anything you learned about interacting with the Bible—or the tools you used along the way—that you want to remember?

_____

_____

_____

_____

_____

EXPERIMENT 2: Read for Intent

First, circle one of these Bible books:
- 1 Timothy
- 2 Timothy
- Philemon
- 2 John
- 3 John

Here's what those books have in common: They're all short and were written with specific audiences in mind.

This experiment involves reading an entire book in one sitting (see why short matters?) and seeing if you can identify the intent of the author.

But when you read your book, read it *out loud*—so you not only see the words but hear them as well. Trust us: It's a different experience.

When you've finished reading, answer these questions:

• What do you think the author's intent was in writing the book?

• What were the most important topics covered in the book?

• And in what ways did the book speak to you?

Jot your thoughts here:

_____

_____

_____

_____

Finished? Now if you'd like to see if others agree with you, consult a commentary or two. But if your answers don't match what the commentary writers say, that's okay—because there are no right answers to these questions.

There are *popular* answers, yes, but perhaps God is saying something to you that he hasn't said to others. Maybe he's showing you something that's especially for you.

Be open to that—because friends do that sort of thing for each other.

And if you discovered this was a non-boring way to engage the Bible, read the other Bible books listed on page 80 in other sittings. And then head to the psalms; they're bite-sized chunks of text that work perfectly for this.

Except for Psalm 119, that is. *That* one's a bruiser—176 verses—but totally worth it.

EXPERIMENT 3: *Lectio Divina*

That's Latin for "sacred reading," by the way—and it's an ancient approach to reading the Bible.

It involves four steps:

Lectio: Select a passage—a chapter of the Bible, perhaps—and read it slowly. Don't worry about analyzing the meaning of the text. Just let your mind linger on individual words and phrases as you read. Let the passage sink in; consider reading it several times.

Meditatio: This is a meditation phase of the process. As you read, you're likely to find that you're drawn to one specific phrase or section of the passage. Zero in on it, reading it again and again, letting the words form a familiar pattern in your mind.

Oratio: Repeatedly recite aloud the phrase you were drawn to. You're creating a calm space in your mind and heart and letting the phrase God brought most vividly to your attention fill that space. It's prayer— only you're using God's words rather than your own.

Contemplatio: If you feel yourself drifting into meditation, go with it. Be silent and still, and be in the presence of God.

Unless you happen to be a member of a monastic order, this may be a new approach to experiencing the Bible. It may be uncomfortable because you're setting aside the typical goal of studying a passage; instead, you're just letting it roll over and through you. *Lectio divina* takes some practice, but it's worth trying several times before you decide if it's for you.

But what do you think now that you've tried it once?

Jot down your thoughts. And be sure to describe how you felt, too.

_____

_____

_____

_____

_____

EXPERIMENT 4: Audio Input

Maybe you're not much of a reader.

Or maybe you are, but you're also someone who spends a lot of time behind the wheel where reading isn't exactly encouraged.

Do this: Take in the Bible through your ears. Download an audio version of the Bible to your phone or tablet (a New Living Translation version is available for free through iTunes), and listen as you drive, do housework, fix dinner, or pay the bills.

Some people find this freeing and helpful. Others struggle to pay sufficient attention to what they're hearing and find the experience frustrating.

See how it works for you.

After you've given it a try for a day or two, jot down your thoughts about the experience. Is this something you'll do on a regular basis? Why or why not?

EXPERIMENT 5: Write It

A challenge people sometimes face when reading the Bible is a tendency for their minds to wander.

They start reading, and about three minutes in, suddenly remember Sheila's birthday party is in two weeks so there's a present to buy and a scarf would be nice—not one of those scratchy wool ones but something silky...and patterned...floral, maybe?

Now, what was Moses saying?

This experiment will help you slow down and focus. To concentrate on each and every word of the Bible passage in front of you. To consider the flow of ideas as the text flows from one paragraph to the next.

You'll need a Bible, a pen, a few pages of lined paper, and a comfortable place to sit and write. When you've got what you need and you're seated, keep reading.

Glad you're back.

What you'll do is open your Bible and begin copying what you see in the text onto your lined paper. And as you write, think about what you're writing.

If, as a child, you were ever forced to write a sentence a hundred times as punishment, you'll *hate* this experiment...at least at first. But keep in mind the goal is anything *but* punishment; it's to help you deeply consider whatever passage you're copying. To dial you in. To engage you.

So put some relaxing music on, and fire up the tea kettle. Let this be a time for relaxing, reflecting, and considering how God might be making himself known through the words you're writing.

Invite your Friend to speak to you as you think about nothing but his words.

You can copy any passage you'd like, or take a chance and just let your Bible fall open and begin there. Write as long as you'd like—a few sentences or a few pages—and then pause to read what you've written.

The penmanship is yours, but the words are God's.

What is he saying to you?

Jot down what you learn.

EXPERIMENT 6: Rewrite It

Time to write your *own* version of the Bible: The Authorized [Your Name Here] Version.

In this experiment you'll read a section of the Bible and then paraphrase what you've read. Don't worry about spelling or punctuation; you're the only one who'll be reading what you write. And if you change your mind about how you want to summarize a thought, just cross out what you wrote and revise it.

Start with the book of Luke, and paraphrase the first chapter.

When you've finished writing, read what you've written and answer this question: What insights did you gain from this exercise? Were there things you saw for the first time? things that seemed to take on new meaning?

Jot those insights here.

EXPERIMENT 7: Be There

For this experiment, select a narrative passage in the Bible, one that describes unfolding events.

For purposes of this experiment, we suggest Mark 5:1-20.

Do this: Read the passage to get the gist of who all was on the scene: disciples, Jesus, a demon-possessed man, Legion, a herd of pigs, herdsmen, and townspeople.

Now, with your imagination in fifth gear, read the passage again, drilling into the story from the perspective of the disciples.

What do they see as these events unfold? What do they hear? Do they splash to shore or step onto dry land? As they see the demon-possessed man running toward them, do they tense up? reach for swords? How are they feeling?

See the story unfold and then read it again—this time from the perspective of Jesus. What does Jesus hear? see? smell? taste? When he catches the eye of the demon-possessed man, what's the look in Jesus' eyes?

Sometimes it's helpful to actually stand and move around a room, placing yourself in the action.

Cycle through all of the characters in this encounter—including the pigs. Just make sure nobody walks in as you're on all fours, grunting your way toward the cliff.

When you've finished, pause to jot your thoughts about how you felt about this exercise. What was it like to engage the Bible in this way?

And if you hear some gentle laughter in the distance, perhaps that's Jesus commenting on his friend's portrayal of a pig.

EXPERIMENT 8: Sketch It

Though avid readers might argue otherwise, words aren't the only way to enter into the Bible. For people more moved by art, visuals are an excellent portal into the Bible.

So give this a try.

First, find a child willing to loan you a children's story Bible. These are collections of Bible stories that often emphasize art more than text.

One outstanding example is Group's *Friends With God Story Bible*. Winsome art, memorable text (all stories are told in the first person, as if a Bible character is speaking), and even fun devotional material are provided with each story.

Read the text, but focus more on the artwork. Drift into and through the pages, letting God speak to you there. Notice the expressions on the faces in the illustrations; read the emotion on those faces. Ask God to reveal something new to you as you run your fingers over the artwork.

See how switching off the analytical side of your brain opens up insights in that part of your brain that's drawn to art.

When you've tried this, capture how it felt by sketching something on page 92.

EXPERIMENT 9: Change Venues

It's a simple thing, but it can make a world of difference when it comes to reading the Bible: Change venues.

For example, if you're accustomed to reading inside, find a park bench and read there. Even better, plant yourself under a tree in a meadow.

If you normally read just before going to bed, read during your lunch hour instead. Shake yourself out of your reading rut; it's amazing how that can give you fresh eyes for the Bible.

Or for anything else, for that matter.

Routine can be wonderful, but it can also dull your enthusiasm. You're in a friendship with God! That's something to be excited about!

So don't limit yourself to a routine that drains all the spontaneity from your friendship. Try reading in different places, at different times, and in different ways. See what happens.

Once you've tried it, jot your thoughts about whether it was useful.

EXPERIMENT 10: Explain It

Ken teaches in his church's Sunday school and loves it, in part because it's transformed how he reads the Bible.

"We use a prepared curriculum," Ken says, "but I always do some extra prep so I'm sure I can explain Bible passages to second-graders in ways they can understand."

Ken says that forces him to dig deep into the passages he's teaching, boiling them down to their essential truths.

"When I know what's happening in a passage well enough to explain it, that's when I know I've let it sink into my heart, too," says Ken.

You may not be teaching a gaggle of second-graders, but you can benefit from Ken's discovery: Take the time to explain what you've read in the Bible to someone else.

And even if you don't have an audience, give this a try: Imagine yourself in front of people, cats, or cactuses—anyone or anything. Then share what you've read and what it meant to you.

Even if you don't see him, someone is listening, and that's God himself.

And he's having a great time.

After trying this a few times, make a note below about whether this is a technique you want to try again.

_____

_____

_____

_____

_____

EXPERIMENT 11: Meditate

Meditation has gotten a bad reputation because it's closely associated with Eastern religions. But it's *also* associated with reducing anxiety, sharpening focus, and improving concentration.

So, you know, it's not *all* bad.

The problem isn't with meditation itself; it's on what (or whom) you focus while meditating. And, in your case, it won't be to empty yourself of ego or ambition, or to somehow tap into your inner self.

You'll be meditating on God's Word, which can be a remarkably powerful way to experience the Bible.

And you won't be the first person to give this a try.

When Joshua was about to lead the Israelites into the Promised Land, God gave him some advice, including this: "Study this Book of Instruction continually. Meditate on it day and night so you will be sure to obey everything written in it. Only then will you prosper and succeed in all you do" (Joshua 1:8).

God isn't suggesting that Joshua haul around a yoga mat to do his meditating. God is suggesting something else, and it's something you can do, too.

The implication is that Joshua will become familiar with the instructions given by God and refer to them often, mulling them over, perhaps repeating them throughout the day as opportunities arise.

The goal is to remember what God wants and to act in accordance with God's expressed desires.

Please don't set for yourself the task of reciting the entire Bible every day. But *do* select a few phrases and revisit them while at red lights...while waiting for your computer to reboot...or when glancing in a mirror.

Try this: Read 1 Thessalonians 5:16-18 at least 10 times. Get the gist, if not the exact wording, so you can repeat it aloud.

Then rephrase the passage in your own words. That confirms you have the concepts down cold.

Now pick a trigger that will remind you to repeat the passage aloud throughout the day. One friend uses bathroom breaks as a reminder, but, well…

Give this kind of meditation a day or two, and then jot how it's worked for you. Did you find yourself being challenged by the truth you were remembering? Did it pop into your head when you found yourself discouraged or under pressure?

EXPERIMENT 12: Question What You Read

Krista has two Bibles but allows people to see only one of them.

"There's one I carry around and one I keep under a stack of magazines next to the couch," she says. In the second Bible she circles any passage she comes across that she either disagrees with or doesn't understand.

"There are lots of circles," Krista admits. "I've got lots of questions."

That's probably true of most Bible readers, but Krista has the courage—sort of—to admit it.

She's courageous enough to ask questions but so far hasn't been courageous enough to show her second Bible to anyone who might be able to help her address her questions.

She's afraid that others will think her a second-rate Christian if she doesn't *get* everything in the Bible. And what might they say if she outs herself as an occasional doubter?

They'll probably say, "Welcome to the club," that's what.

Krista is deeply engaged with the Bible, comparing what it says to what she observes in life and herself. And not everything lines up. Forgiving someone again and again, for instance. Doesn't that just lead to continuing abuse and codependency?

Here's an experiment for you: Read any book of the Bible you choose except 3 John (15 verses…come on, get serious…) and circle what you either disagree with or don't understand.

Then go back to each of the passages you circled, one at a time. Ask God to make clear what those passages mean; you may clear up simple misunderstandings with a bit of prayer and thinking.

But the knotty stuff—the places your circles can't be dismissed—there you can use help. Take your Bible to a friend who's further along in the faith and ask if he or she can offer you some insight.

But approach both God and your more seasoned friend humbly. Ask your questions with a heartfelt desire to understand, not debate.

It may be that what you've you circled is precisely an area of your life Jesus wants to transform.

Once you've read a book, circling as you go, ask God who to talk with about your concerns.

Then pick up your phone and make the call.

BONUS EXPERIMENT 13: *Lectio Continua*

This is a continuous reading through one book of the Bible, first verse to last.

It's not how most people interact with the Bible these days, either at home or at church. We've largely gone to a *Lectio Selecta* approach—picking passages from throughout the Bible that seem to address a specific topic.

It's not a bad idea to focus on what the Bible says about finances, say, or marriage.

But there's something good about reading a book of the Bible in its entirety, too.

Nothing is out of context. It's easier to sense the author's intent and follow the author's logic.

It was the pattern of first-century synagogues to unroll a scroll of Scripture and read a portion. Then, on the next Sabbath, the reader picked up where he'd left off. It's likely that the early church, steeped in tradition, did the same thing.

If they found value in taking a long view of a passage—of reading entire books all the way through—perhaps there's value for you, too.

So pick a book. One of the four Gospels, perhaps, or the book of Romans. Read it in as few sittings as practical, given your time and ability to concentrate. Pay attention to the flow of the writing and what the author is trying to say to you as he reaches out across the centuries.

And—as always—be asking Jesus what he has to show you about himself...and about you.

JUST CURIOUS:

ARE THERE TIMES I *SHOULDN'T* READ THE BIBLE?

Yes, there are.

There are times the very best thing you can do is to close your Bible and set it aside. Which is strange advice to find in a book about how to read the Bible.

But remember: *The Bible is all about relationship.* Above all else—above being an account of God's faithfulness or history or poetry or a gathering place for superior advice—it's about relationship.

About God calling you his friend…and your response to that call.

As strange as it might sound, the Bible can at times get in the way of that friendship. It can become a substitute for more direct communication with God.

Our friend Matt was once going through a rough patch in his friendship with God. A lingering illness, a growing dissatisfaction with his job, a drift in his marriage, a sense that nothing would ever get better. It all added up to a deepening resentment toward God.

Yet Matt never missed a morning devotional time. He'd dutifully open a Bible and plod ahead in his reading program, sometimes hardly noticing the words on the page.

One morning he looked up to see his wife leaning in the kitchen doorway.

She walked over to him, reached down, and shut his Bible. And then she said something Matt has never forgotten.

"Relationships are messy, and you don't like messes," she said. "So you've settled for the literature instead of the relationship."

Her words cut Matt to his core because they were stunningly, beautifully, horribly true.

Matt's Bible reading was his way of keeping God at arm's length. He wasn't cutting off his relationship with God, but he wasn't dealing with the elephants parading around the room, either.

"What I needed at that point in my life wasn't to read more about God. It was to go stand in a field and scream at God. To tell him how bitter and disappointed I was with myself, with life, with him. To let it all pour out and then just fall to my knees and let him hold me."

Those moments. Those are the moments to close your Bible and wade into the mess. To have the hard conversation with God directly, without filtering it through his book.

Don't worry—in time God will draw you back to the Bible because there's Life there. He's there.

But he's also in that field, waiting for you.

Is there a conversation you need to have *with* God before you settle for one more devotion *about* him?

PAUSE TO PONDER

Where's the messiness in your friendship with God? Write or draw your response below:

What is the hard conversation with Jesus you've put off but feel nudged to have now?

HELP! HOW DO I READ THE BIBLE...
WHEN PEOPLE ARGUE ABOUT
WHETHER IT'S EVEN TRUE?

The Bible is true. All of it.

How much of it is *literally* true? That's been debated for centuries.

The Bible makes some fairly spectacular claims. It asserts that God exists. That God created the universe from nothing. That, at God's command, seas part, the sun stands still, and dead people rise from their graves.

It asks you to believe in things you can't see and live in ways that sometimes stretch you to the breaking point.

And some people believe that every word of the Bible is literally true.

"That's how I was raised," says Jason. "Our favorite bumper sticker was 'God said it. I believe it. That settles it.' We spent as much time in church mocking scientists as we spent talking about Jesus."

An uncompromising, unquestioning conviction that the Bible is word-for-word literally true defined Jason's early experience with the Bible. And he held that position until it was shaken at, of all places, a Bible college.

"In an Old Testament course, we learned that ancient Hebrew literature often took liberties with details in a story because details didn't matter as much as the point of the story. Except in the Bible. In the Bible, six days of Creation meant six 24-hour days. Samson's claim that he killed a thousand men with a donkey's jawbone meant there were literally a thousand guys laid out on the ground."

When Jason raised his hand to question a literal interpretation or two, he was met with lectures about the weakness of his faith.

But Jason had already turned a corner.

"I realized I didn't care if every logistical detail in the Bible was accurate," he says. "I cared about God. About knowing God and seeing who he was revealed to be in all of the Bible narratives."

It's probably no surprise Jason was eventually invited to leave the college. And that he found a home elsewhere, with Christians who took a less rigorous view of whether each word in the Bible was to be taken literally.

Please hear this: We're not lobbying one way or the other about how literally you should read the Bible. We're simply raising the question because what you think matters.

The Bible portrays itself as representing God's take on moral issues. If that's the case, then the Bible has some authority in the life of God's friends—people like you. You'll want to let it influence your thinking and decision-making.

But if the Bible's just a collection of instructive stories, on a par with *Aesop's Fables,* then while it may be interesting and informative, there's no harm in ignoring it.

So you've got to decide: How seriously will you take the Bible and what it says? We ask, not to make you feel guilty, but because the question is a good-sized elephant wandering around the room.

We suggest you chat with Jesus about the question. Have the conversation, and see where you land.

We *can* tell you this: People lined up in the camp where Jason was raised—the every-word-is-to-be-taken-literally camp—often suggest their view of the Bible is supported by these five points:

• *The Bible is full of fulfilled prophecy.* Many prophecies in the Old Testament books about the coming Messiah were fulfilled in the person of Jesus. Those prophecies were to be taken literally; that argues for taking the rest of the text literally, too.

• *That the Bible exists at all proves it's true.* The Bible had a tenuous beginning, yet it survived. In spite of attempts to suppress the Bible, it has thrived. All of this is evidence of God's blessing on its truth.

• *Its text is unified.* Given the wide range of authors and the different times and cultures in which the 66 books of the Bible were written, they're remarkably consistent and cohesive. They tell one story and do so with authority, evidence they're God-breathed and true.

• *Archeology and geology support it.* When the Bible pinpoints a location in the ancient world, excavations inevitably confirm the Bible's accuracy and trustworthiness. If those facts are correct, so is everything else.

And then there's the evidence Jason finds most compelling:

• *It changes lives.* When people come with open hearts to the God described in the Bible, remarkable things happen. As they accept God's friendship and choose to follow Jesus, they're transformed. That simply wouldn't happen if the Bible weren't truly the Word of the living God.

Is the Bible true? Yes—because God is true. And God invites you into the Bible because it's one place he'll meet you and deepen your friendship.

God invites you to "taste and see that the Lord is good" (Psalm 34:8).

So pull up a seat at the table—it's time to do a bit of tasting.

PAUSE TO PONDER

People can (and will) argue about interpreting the Bible all day long.

But nobody can argue with changed lives.

So pause and think about this: In what ways has knowing God changed your life? And what part, if any, has reading the Bible played in that change?

Jot your story here…

How do you feel about what you've written? If your friendship with God could fuel any change in your life, what change would you want more than any other?

Describe it below. Then invite Jesus to enter into your situation.

EXPERIMENT 1: Ask God

You saw this coming, didn't you?

If anyone can tell you all about the Bible, it's God. And, since the two of you are friends, he won't get upset if you ask him: Exactly how literally should you take some of the events described in the Bible?

Ask humbly, and listen carefully for his answer. It may not come immediately, and that's okay. You both have plenty of time.

When you get a sense of what you're hearing, jot it below and then look at what you wrote on the previous page.

Has your understanding shifted? In what ways?

EXPERIMENT 2: Replacement Bookmark

Jason described how he was raised as a bumper sticker: "God said it. I believe it. That settles it."

How would you sum up your beliefs about the Bible in a bumper-sticker slogan? Something short—but accurate. Extra points if it's catchy.

Jot your bumper sticker below:

HELP! HOW DO I READ THE BIBLE... WHEN THERE ARE SO MANY CONTRADICTIONS IN IT?

That's a charge that's leveled against the Bible often, and it stops lots of Bible readers in their tracks.

They're zipping along, feeling great about their friendship with God and how it's being deepened by exploring the Bible. Then a friend or family member raises a warning eyebrow and says, "Well, sure...but how about all those contradictions in the Bible?"

And then that's that. Game over.

This concern is closely related to a conversation about whether the Bible can be taken literally, but given how often this issue arises among Bible readers, it's worth tackling on its own.

First, to be fair, there's a big difference between a *contradiction* and a *discrepancy*.

A *contradiction* is a total lack of compatibility between two descriptions of the same event.

For example, if you leave two young boys in the same kitchen with one off-limits cookie, you'll likely hear a contradiction when you ask them to explain what became of the cookie.

Each will claim the other ate it while your back was turned. That's a contradiction because only one of the stories can possibly be true.

A *discrepancy* is just a difference in how they tell the same story.

The first boy may point to the second and say the cookie-snatcher not only ate the cookie but also smacked his lips and grinned as he did so. The second boy—the one with cookie crumbs on his chin—may admit he ate the cookie but claim he's deeply sorry and ate it with great reluctance. He sees the error of his ways.

That's a discrepancy: Both boys agree who committed the crime, but the details of said crime vary.

And there are *lots* of discrepancies in the Bible.

One event described four times, by four Bible writers, is the crucifixion of Jesus. Each mentioned a sign nailed over Jesus' head on the cross, but each account of what the sign said is different.

Matthew reported the sign said, "This is Jesus, the King of the Jews" (Matthew 27:37).

Mark quotes the sign as saying, "The King of the Jews" (Mark 15:26).

Luke describes the wording this way: "This is the King of the Jews" (Luke 23:38).

And here's what John writes: "Jesus of Nazareth, the King of the Jews" (John 19:19).

Is this a contradiction? No, it's a discrepancy. Same event, four slight variations in how it's described.

The various wordings don't change the meaning of the message. And John offers a clue as to what might explain the discrepancy: The sign spelling out Jesus' crime was written in three different languages: Hebrew, Latin, and Greek (John 19:20).

Plenty of room for discrepancy there…and plenty more when you factor in we're reading Bibles translated by scholars who had to make wording choices.

There are people who love nothing more than pointing out discrepancies like this in the Bible. They see them as evidence that the Bible—and its message—is flawed.

And there are just as many people who feel the need to carpet-bomb the internet with plausible explanations of those discrepancies, who seem ready to defend to the death the idea that the Bible is infallible.

There's an entire field of study—apologetics— dedicated to defending the Christian faith, including the Bible.

But...why?

Why the frantic need to prove that the Bible contains no contradictions or mistakes? What's fueling that fire?

There are loads of reasons, but here's the one that may matter most: We want to know we can trust the Bible. That it really is the inspired Word of God. If it's riddled with mistakes and inaccuracies, its credibility is called into question.

If the Bible isn't credible, then what it says about God isn't reliable. And you're wasting your time reading it.

So...is the Bible trustworthy? Is that really God's voice you hear ringing through its pages or the echo of authors simply sharing their opinions? Is that long shadow you see stretching across thousands of events God's shadow—or something else?

Here's the good news: The Bible is trustworthy.

Almost all of the "contradictions" cited in the Bible are discrepancies. They're easily explained. And those that can't be explained are usually the fruit of faulty translation or a misunderstanding of a literary reference.

When the Bible's references to specific places, times, or dates are attacked, you can relax there, too.

The fact that nobody has yet uncovered an ancient city doesn't mean it wasn't there or won't be found next year. Objections to logistics mentioned in the Bible have been steadily whittled away over the years; more will be resolved in years to come.

If you're detail-oriented and want to dive into the deep end of the apologetics pool, that's your privilege. Just don't lose sight of two truths:

You can trust that Jesus is waiting to connect with you in the pages of the Bible.

And it's your call as to whether you'll give him the opportunity.

PAUSE TO PONDER

What's something in the Bible you're 100 percent certain is true?

Jot it here...

How do you know it's true? What fuels your certainty? Is it something you believe…that you can objectively prove…that you've experienced?

Please explain here…

_____

_____

_____

_____

_____

_____

God speaks to you through your whole person— your emotions as well as your thoughts. Every growing friendship is like that; it's more than a rational equation. It's a living thing, and it moves forward at the speed of trust.

Ask God what the next step is in your friendship with him.

Where is trust taking you?

EXPERIMENT 1: Discrepancy Practice

This experiment is going to cost you—but it will be worth it.

Invite a friend to lunch. Explain you'll even pick up the tab…if your friend is willing to help you with this experiment.

Bring paper and a couple of pens. Order lunch. Enjoy lunch. Then, after the dishes are cleared away, hand your friend paper and a pen. Ask your friend to describe what's happened since you walked into the restaurant.

Do the same—and give yourselves eight minutes to write.

When you've finished writing, read aloud what you wrote and have your friend do the same.

You didn't both include the same details, did you?

Your friend may have described what you ate, and you might have described the waitstaff who took care of you. Your friend may not have even mentioned the name of the restaurant, while you might have given its GPS coordinates and a full review for posting online.

Whose description is right?

The answer: Both. Your descriptions complement each other, but they're by no means identical. And you *did* share the same experience, even if your descriptions aren't the same.

Talk with your friend about discrepancies in the Bible—and elsewhere in life. See where that conversation takes you.

And tip your waiter well. He's wondering what's wrong with the two of you.

> **Always be joyful. Never stop praying. Be thankful in all circumstances, for this is God's will for you who belong to Christ Jesus.**
>
> *1 Thessalonians 5:16–18*

HELP! HOW DO I READ THE BIBLE... WHEN I'M DOING THIS ALONE?

First, you aren't really alone. The Holy Spirit is gently guiding you, and you're meeting your friend Jesus in the pages of the Bible.

But when it comes to people plopped down next to you on the sofa, cheering you on, we get your point. It's encouraging to share a project with others, to be at each other's sides, cheering each other on.

That's one reason Bible studies are popular. A group of people reading the same passages at the same time, then reviewing what they've read, have built-in cheerleaders. Group studies provide structure, accountability, and if you join the right Bible study, a steady supply of snacks.

But there's that word again: *study*.

Is studying the text of the Bible what you most want to do? Or are you more drawn to staying focused on connecting with Jesus as you explore the Bible?

If you're hungry for structure but want to move past the literature and deeper into the relationship, we suggest this: Get the best of both worlds.

Spread the word you'd like to either create or join a "Joining Jesus Group," that is, a group that will dig into the Bible but from a slightly unusual angle: You'll focus on seeking Jesus' heart rather than dissecting his quotes.

The difference isn't *what* you read but *how* you read it. And *why*.

Your group will come to Bible passages asking questions that are far different from those that arise in typical Bible studies.

Rather than reading about something Jesus did and then talking about what he did, you'll ask, "Why do you suppose Jesus did that? How do you see his heart revealed in what happened?" You'll enter into the passages hungrier for relationship than Bible facts.

And when you do that, Jesus will be quick to meet you there.

PAUSE TO PONDER

If you've experienced organized Bible studies in the past, describe that experience below. What about being part of a study was most enjoyable or helpful? What was just so-so or actually discouraging?

How would you feel about being part of an organized group if the emphasis was on encountering the heart of Jesus? When has an experience of reading the Bible in the context of a community affected your heart more than your head, and why?

EXPERIMENT 1: A Group of Two

Ask a Christian friend to join you in a two-person Joining Jesus Group. Set a time limit from the very start—no more than three one-hour meetings before evaluating if you both want to continue.

Choose passages in the Bible to read together (we suggest you begin where Jesus is most clearly visible—in the Gospels) and then talk about your responses to the following questions:

• Why do you suppose Jesus did that?

• How do you see his heart revealed in what happened?

• How might what we discovered shape our relationship with Jesus?

• How might it shape our relationship with each other?

And resist the temptation to quickly shift to applying what you discover to your own lives. Instead, *stay focused on Jesus,* digging deeply, giving him space to reveal himself to you. That almost always happens when you take time to ask a question a second or third time, not hurrying to get a "right answer" but instead listening to hear what Jesus has to say.

After you and your friend have met several times, jot down your thoughts about how this experiment worked for you…

_____

_____

_____

_____

_____

If you've found Jesus is meeting you as you read, consider inviting others to join you for the next few meetings. He'll be happy to meet them, too.

EXPERIMENT 2: Hiking With Jesus

When Mary and Fran started taking walks around the neighborhood together a few years ago, they were mostly seeking exercise.

"Middle age is where cellulite waits to ambush you," laughs Fran. "Mary and I were friends and in the same small group at church, so we decided to get in a little exercise to burn off calories. We knew if we did it together neither of us could back out."

After a few half-hour walks, Mary arrived at Fran's house one day with shattering news: Her son was divorcing, and she was losing access to her grandchildren. That topic consumed the walk—several walks—and then Fran suggested they pray together as they walked.

Which led, in a few weeks, to the two women poring through Scripture to see what, if anything, the Bible had to say about dealing with loss.

"It turns out there was plenty," says Fran.

The friends are still walking and talking several times each week. But now their conversations are almost always comparing notes about what they've read in the Bible. It's a free-wheeling, wide-ranging discussion driven by what's happening in their lives and which passages have struck them most powerfully.

"Sometimes it feels as if Jesus is walking right along with us," says Fran. "Those are the best days."

Is there something in that story for you?

What would happen if you and a Christian friend took walks together, discussing what you've read in the Bible? Not for purposes of teaching, but of reaching—reaching deep into honest conversation and into the long pauses that give Jesus a chance to join you on your journey.

Who can you call to ask to share a walk or two?

When you have someone in mind, call and read the person Mary and Fran's story. See if he or she has enthusiasm for an experiment like this.

Yes? Pull on your hiking shoes.

No? Call the next person who comes to mind.

After you've taken a few walks, jot down how this experiment played out for you. Perhaps you've found a Bible-reading partner.

"

All Scripture
is inspired by God
and is useful to teach us
what is true and to make us
realize what is wrong in our
lives. It corrects us when we
are wrong and teaches us
to do what is right.

"

2 Timothy 3:16

HELP! HOW DO I READ THE BIBLE...
WHEN I DON'T HAVE ALL THOSE
NIFTY STUDY TOOLS?

When it comes to resources designed to help you engage with and understand the Bible, there's never been a better time than now.

Why? Because those resources are less expensive and more readily available now than ever before. Basic versions of everything described in this chapter can be found online, often for free.

That's no small thing, as anyone who went to seminary before the internet ruled the earth will tell you. Not so very long ago pastors in training had to spend thousands of dollars to equip a personal library. Now the same reference material can be had at a fraction of the cost with a few clicks of the mouse.

Keep in mind you don't really need any of these resources, not if your goal in reading the Bible is to deepen your friendship with God. But the more time you spend in the Bible, the more curious you're likely to become, and these tools can help you get a fuller understanding of the text.

Just make sure you keep your focus on God rather than the tools. As long as you continue reading for relationship, these tools can shine fresh light on passages you encounter.

Here's a quick jog through 10 tools you might consider adding to your bookshelf, or if you're thrifty, consulting online.

Bible Dictionary

This usually looks less like a dictionary than an old-school encyclopedia. You'll find brief articles about the people, places, customs, and events portrayed in the Bible. It's a useful tool if you'd like to better understand the world in which the Bible arrived.

Jesus' earthly father, Joseph, was a carpenter...but what does that mean? What was daily life like for a carpenter or tax collector or fisherman? The entries in a Bible dictionary can tell you.

A tip if you're considering bringing home a Bible dictionary: Consider buying a children's pictorial edition. Many do a superb job of providing clear, simple information that adds depth to your Bible reading.

Plus, there are pictures, and we like pictures.

Bible Encyclopedia

This is essentially a Bible dictionary on steroids. It deals with the same sort of content as a Bible dictionary, but in far greater depth. These are usually multi-volume sets of books and are as expensive as they are impressive on the shelf.

Bible Atlas

This is a collection of maps that shows the Middle East as it appeared during the events described in the Bible. It's especially useful when you're trying to picture the traveling ministry of Jesus or the missionary journeys of Paul.

With an atlas you can quickly understand the scope of a journey that's described in the Bible. It's information that the original recipients of the books of the Bible would already have had—they knew where Bethlehem was in relationship to Jerusalem. But you might not know whether 5, 50, or 500 miles separate the two locations.

The best atlases include maps describing the region as it appeared in both Old and New Testament times. And they show not just the location of cities, but also the political boundaries so you can see which powers ruled which territories.

Maps range from simple descriptions to finely detailed, topographical, geo-political maps you could use to plot an attack on the Old Testament city of your choice. You could probably settle for simpler maps; they'll tell you pretty much everything you want to know.

Bible Commentaries

Generally written by one or more scholars or pastors, commentaries are verse-by-verse, section-by-section dissections of biblical books. Their chief benefit is that research into the historical, cultural, and literary context of a given book has been pulled together in one convenient spot.

But because anyone can write a commentary, they differ widely in their accuracy, readability, and thoroughness. Plus, some commentary writers blur the line between background information and interpretation and find ways to shoehorn in their own theology.

Proceed with caution.

Concordance

If you've ever wondered where the people who used to research and write telephone books ended up, you now have your answer: They create concordances.

A concordance is essentially a detailed listing of every word found in the Bible—arranged alphabetically and cross-referenced so, if you're looking to see where the word *friend* appears in the Bible, you'll have all those references in one handy spot.

Well, not exactly handy, as you'll have to look up every reference in a Bible to see how the word is used. And you won't know how relevant each listing is because concordance writers tend to not rank relevance; they report the facts and only the facts. Any given reference can be a passage all about friends, a casual reference to a friend, or somewhere in the middle.

Also, concordances are often tightly tied to specific versions of the Bible. A concordance that's keyed to the King James Version will list words that never appear in other Bible versions.

You can bypass that peculiarity and add an entirely new level of complexity by finding a concordance tied to Greek and Hebrew words that appear in the Bible.

This is a tool generally used by theologians, pastors, and more serious Bible students—the sort of students with a term paper in their immediate future.

It's not uncommon for a basic concordance to be included in a Bible, so don't head to the bookstore to buy one unless you plan to do specific, significant research.

Bible Handbook

If your Bible came with an owner's manual, this would be it. It's a combination of background information on each book of the Bible and a brief commentary, all rolled into one usually succinct package.

Like nearly all of the tools described here, Bible handbooks come in varying degrees of depth and complexity.

Expository Dictionary

This is essentially a cheat sheet for those of us who want to study the meaning of Hebrew and Greek words without learning the languages.

Parallel Bible

This is an entire Bible with multiple translations printed side by side, the preferred Bible for anyone who likes comparing how several translators handled a particular passage.

As you might imagine, it makes for one Very Large Bible (and an expensive one at that), and it's only slightly less work to carry it around than to have multiple versions of the Bible at hand.

Also, with most versions of the Bible available online, you can easily do electronically what a parallel Bible does physically.

Dictionary of Biblical Imagery

What a Bible dictionary does for explaining history and culture in Bible times, a biblical imagery dictionary does for the themes, images, and figures of speech that appear in the Bible. This can be especially helpful when you're curious about the "why" behind the "what" of a name, phrase, or metaphor.

Interlinear Bible

If you exiled a Greek scholar, Hebrew scholar, and an English major to a dessert island for a decade, an Interlinear Bible would be waiting when you came to pick them up. It's a word-by-word, literal translation of the Bible from Greek or Hebrew into English. While not an easy read, if you're willing to sacrifice readability for accuracy, here's the ticket.

By the way, pick another English major because it's "*desert* island," not "*dessert* island." Someone who'd buy an interlinear Bible would have caught that.

Again—none of these tools is necessary to encounter God in the Bible. But they can all be useful in helping you grasp the culture and context into which Bible books were introduced. They can fill in the shading of your understanding and answer lots of questions.

Keep in mind that the scholars who translated your Bible—especially if it was translated in the past hundred years—had access to all these tools. They did the hard work of mastering languages and debating word choices. They hammered out text that balances accuracy and readability.

In short, with nearly every Bible translation, you're in good hands.

PAUSE TO PONDER

As you read this list of tools, which one or two sounded as if they'd be most helpful, given how you read the Bible?

May we make a suggestion? (It doesn't really matter if you say no. We're going to make one anyway.)

If you have room in your life for just one tool, make it a Bible dictionary. Having the background about everyday life in first-century Palestine fleshes out your ability to imagine what was happening when Jesus interacted with people. You'll almost be able to feel the spray on your face when you're reading about storms on the Sea of Galilee and hear the crowds elbowing their way to the Temple when Jesus and his disciples were in Jerusalem celebrating a holiday.

No, we don't sell Bible dictionaries. But just thinking about what a difference they've made in helping us enter into Bible events makes us want to buy another one.

" The highest view of the Scriptures is not the one that seeks to make an idol of the Bible (biblicism), but the one that allows the biblical text to exalt Christ as the living Word over all creation. The Word became flesh, not ink. "

—*David D. Flowers*

WHY DO I GET EXTRA POINTS FOR WRITING IN THE BIBLE?

Point of order: You get extra points for writing in *your* Bible. Write in someone *else's* Bible, and things may not end well for you.

Angie is an adult now, but back when she was in a high school youth group, she always "borrowed" her mother's Bible to carry to group meetings.

"It was in a huge, leather carrying case," Angie says. "Inside was a notebook, a couple of pens, and a Bible that was highlighted in a half-dozen colors. And notes everywhere—in the margins, on sheets of paper stuck between pages of the Bible, on hundreds of sticky notes.

"Whenever I pulled out that Bible, everyone assumed I was the holiest kid in six counties."

Angie's mother was a serious student of the Bible, and those notes were her personal version of a Bible encyclopedia. When she heard something new in a sermon—a note. When a comment at a women's Bible study shone fresh light on a familiar verse—another note.

And most important of all: When she felt God was speaking to her about something specific—a person, a problem, a prayer concern—Angie's mom made yet another note.

"That Bible represented 20 years of study," Angie remembers. "But it also reflected her spiritual journey. Anyone who read those notes would have a pretty good idea of what she and God had been talking about all that time."

You may not have the same zeal for documenting your journey through the Bible, but Angie's mom was on to something: There's power in remembering what God shows you in the Bible, in jotting down insights or questions that come to mind as you read.

Reading the Bible with a pen in one hand has become so popular that some Bibles are printed with intentionally wide, uncluttered margins just begging to be filled with drawings, doodles, and notes.

It's not sacrilege to write in your Bible. You're simply writing back to someone who's gone to great lengths to write to you.

And whether you write in the Bible itself or tuck a small notebook inside the Bible's back cover instead, Bible journaling has benefits worth considering:

• **You're engaged.** That you come to the Bible ready to take notes means you're expecting to find something noteworthy, expecting to hear from God.

That's far better than yawning through a few chapters of a prescribed reading program just so you can check off your Bible-reading task for the day and move on.

• **You're focused.** We call it the Yellow Volkswagen Principle: Once you start looking for them, you're amazed at how many seem to be out there.

The truth is that when you come to the Bible expecting to see something, you'll generally find it. If you're looking for rules, you'll find them. If you're looking for history, it's there. If you're looking for beautiful language, there's plenty to enjoy.

But if you come expecting to connect with your friend, the God who reveals himself in spectacular ways in every page of the Bible, that's what will leap off the page at you. Keeping *that* focus in mind—how God is showing himself and his heart—will have you filling margins and notebooks with transforming truths.

• **You're creating a reminder.** Your writing becomes a tangible record of what God's saying to you about himself...and you.

When you flip to a passage you've read before, there in the margin may be a summary of how it struck you in the past. You're able to track your spiritual growth, one inky comment at a time.

Journaling your relationship with God *does* come with a caution: Write for yourself, not for the benefit of others.

As with all journaling, honesty and transparency are directly related to how confident you are that no one else will read what you write. When you write with an audience in mind, it's easy to slip into writing to impress them rather than to process what God's saying to you.

If the prospect of your teenage daughter spiriting your Bible off to her youth group—where a dozen kids could take turns reading your comments aloud—horrifies you, then use journal pages rather than the margins of your Bible to capture your thoughts.

We've provided sample journal pages you're free to copy and use to your heart's content (see pages 146-148). And we recommend using them rather than one of those "Who-What-When-Where-How" pages you can download off the web. Here's why: Ours will focus you on the heart of God.

Whether Jesus healed a blind beggar named Bartimaeus outside Jericho, Jerusalem, or Jacksonville is less important than what he revealed about himself during the encounter. So focus there: on his *heart,* not just the location of his actions.

So, yes: You do get extra points for writing in your Bible…or on a journal page tucked inside it.

And even better, you'll find that as you review and pray about what you write, your friendship with God will grow richer, deeper, and more satisfying.

PAUSE TO PONDER

There are people who journal and love it.

There are people who don't journal and never will.

And then there are people who start journals, get five pages in, and quit.

Which of those descriptions best fits you?

Jot down your past experience with journaling. And yes, if you're rolling your eyes right now, that sends a strong signal that you and journaling haven't been best buddies in the past.

But perhaps it's time to get past any false starts back when you were in middle school and kept a diary under your mattress. If making note of what you discover in the Bible will help move that truth deeper into your heart, isn't it worth a fresh try?

So, again, please describe your past experiences here...

EXPERIMENT 1: Secret Pages

Nothing shuts down journaling like worrying that someone will sneak a peek at what you've written.

So do this: Find a private spot and settle in to write, on a piece of paper, how you're feeling about life today. Be as honest as possible—nobody but you will read what you've written. Don't worry about penmanship, spelling, or punctuation. There's no grade at the end of this exercise.

Finished?

Now empty a metal wastebasket or bucket and find a quiet spot outside. Grab some matches as you head out the door.

When you're sure you're alone, burn what you've written. When the ashes cool, scatter them. Let the breeze take them where it will.

Wait…we lied.

Someone did read what you wrote. Someone was looking over your shoulder the entire time.

And that someone was God.

Since he knows what came pouring out of you onto the paper you burned, why not talk with him about those words scattered around you?

And that's the benefit of journaling: opening up the conversation between you and your friend God. That can be done if you fill the margins of your Bible with your questions, concerns, and insights or if you write and then destroy every word you write.

What matters most isn't what you write. It's the conversation that follows.

Oh, and we were serious: Have the conversation. Don't keep God waiting.

EXPERIMENT 2: Try This

Give these "Heart of God" journal pages a try.

Mark 10:46-52

Date: _____

What does God reveal about himself in this passage, about who he is and what he values?

_____

_____

_____

If God interacted with someone in this passage, what do you think his motivation was? Why?

_____

_____

_____

_____

If God did something in this passage, what do you think he wanted to accomplish? Why?

What does this passage show you about yourself?

How did you feel as you read this passage, and why do you think you responded to it as you did?

What questions does this passage raise for you?

_____

_____

_____

_____

Now enter into a conversation with Jesus. Ask your questions, and see if he leads you to answers.

HELP! HOW DO I READ THE BIBLE... WHEN I'M NOT LEARNING ANYTHING NEW ABOUT GOD ANYWAY?

Ah..."learning anything new."

Like God is a topic to be studied rather than a friend to love.

Like God has nothing more to show you about himself and his kingdom.

Like God isn't interested in your discovering more about who he created you to be.

If you come to the Bible for information, it has an expiration date.

Sooner or later you'll absorb all the data you can handle. You'll have all the facts tucked away that you can possibly learn. Your library of tips and tools will be complete.

But if you're reading for relationship, there's no end to the Bible. It takes you as deep and wide and high as you're willing to go because there's no end to God himself.

And no end to your friendship.

So if you came to this book thinking there would be a graduation party at the end, we're sorry. There's no graduation, but there's something better.

It's an invitation.

You are cordially invited by the God of the universe into a friendship with him that will be endlessly satisfying. And he invites you to meet with him often—including in the pages of the Bible.

We hope you accept the invitation.

Have fun. You're on the adventure of a lifetime.

THE PROBLEM WITH PROOF TEXTING

Pulling Bible verses out of context to make a point can lead to some awkward conclusions.

It can lead to Christians supporting slavery (Colossians 3:22), killing disrespectful kids (Exodus 21:17), and refusing to seek medical treatment (James 5:15).

Consider the following statements—each of which can be "proven" with a Bible verse...

You can do anything— including jumping out of planes without a parachute.

Hey—it's right there in Philippians 4:13: "For I can do everything through Christ, who gives me strength."

Everything means everything, so flying shouldn't be a problem.

Except, if you'll read several pages around this verse, you'll see that Paul is actually writing about how relying on Jesus is helping him cope with being in prison. No promises about parachutes are stated or implied.

Continue beating children until they wise up.

If the following verse was all you knew about how God encourages parents to treat their children, you'd assume beatings were recommended:

"A youngster's heart is filled with foolishness, but physical discipline will drive it far away" (Proverbs 22:15).

That verse has been used to justify corporal punishment and, sadly, even child abuse. Leaving aside whether a swat is biblical, suffice it to say this verse by itself in no way reflects all of God's view about how parents are to value their children.

Context is sometimes larger than just a few pages on either side of a verse; it can be seeing how God handles a topic *throughout* the Bible.

And throughout the Bible, God is quick to temper discipline with love.

Forget praying—just call the psychic hotline instead.

After all, that's what King Saul did in 1 Samuel 28:7:

"Saul then said to his advisers, 'Find a woman who is a medium, so I can go and ask her what to do.'"

Yes, King Saul tracked down a witch and consulted with her. But it got him in a world of trouble with God.

Unless you dig deeper than one verse, you may miss that some decisions documented in the Bible are there as cautionary tales. What people did—including heroes of the faith—was sometimes exactly the *wrong* thing to do.

God promises your life will get easier.

Romans 8:28 is often trotted out to assure Christians any problems they face are about to go away:

"And we know that God causes everything to work together for the good of those who love God and are called according to his purpose for them."

But *good* in this context doesn't equal your life getting easier. God's definition of *good* is that you will become more like Jesus, and sometimes suffering helps that happen.

God endorses smoking.

Assuming you're using the King James Version of the Bible and know that Camel cigarettes have been around more than a hundred years, this may be the best out-of-context proof verse *ever*:

"And Rebekah lifted up her eyes, and when she saw Isaac, she lighted off the camel" (Genesis 24:64, KJV).

Admit it: Wouldn't Rebekah be fetching, fluttering her eyelids at Isaac while firing up a cigarette? Except the context of this event makes it clear that what really happened was that Rebekah dismounted from a camel.

A less dramatic interpretation, perhaps, but far, far, *far* more accurate.

If you're attempting to apply the Bible to a situation in your life, be especially sure you understand what the Bible says *in context*.

THE QUIZ YOU'LL NEVER TAKE

1. Sure you can recite John 3:16 from memory, but what about John 3:*17*? For one point, please recite it aloud.

2. What's the shortest verse in the Bible—and where is it?

3. What's the longest name given to a person in the Bible?

4. If a train leaves Jerusalem traveling toward Bethlehem at a speed of 37.3 miles per hour, and a train traveling toward Jerusalem leaves Bethlehem galloping along at 22.5 miles per hour, how many cubits of gopher wood can one angel juggle while dancing on the head of a pin?

5. According to the New American Standard Bible, what's the last word recorded in the Old Testament?

6. When Moses conducted a census of men over the age of 20 in the first chapter of Numbers, which tribe did he discover was the smallest?

7. The high priest could enter the Holy of Holies only one day a year. What was that day?

8. Using only minor prophets, how many basketball teams can you make?

9. What was the seventh plague God unleashed on Egypt?

10. What was the eleventh plague?

BONUS QUESTIONS

11. Who was David's daddy?

12. Who had a bed 13 feet long and 6 feet wide?
Check your answers on pages 157-158.

QUIZ
ANSWERS

Award yourself one point for each correct answer.

1. Look it up if you don't know it. This is a book about getting you into the Bible, remember?

2. "Jesus wept" (John 11:35).

3. Maher-shalal-hash-baz (Isaiah 8:1). The name means "swift to plunder and quick to carry away" in Hebrew, so it's amazing more pirates didn't later use this name.

4. This question is impossible to answer, so just give yourself a point if you didn't use a bad word while trying to figure it out.

5. "Curse" (Malachi 4:5).

6. Manasseh, assuming we're talking about head count. Nobody knows which tribe was the shortest by height, though our money is on the Teenyites.

7. The Day of Atonement (Yom Kippur).

8. Two. There are 12 minor prophets, so that gives you two teams of five, plus a ref, and Obadiah will be out front taking tickets and running the concessions stand.

9. A thunderstorm of hail (Exodus 9:13-35).

10. Tourists. While not recorded in the Bible, just ask anyone who lives near the pyramids. They'll tell you.

11. Jesse (Matthew 1:6). By the way, if you can recite all of Matthew 1 by heart, listing the lineage from Abraham to Jesus, pronouncing every name correctly, give yourself, like, a *bazillion* points.

12. Wrong—*not* Goliath. It was King Og of Bashan, the last survivor of the giant Rephaites (Deuteronomy 3:11). Good try with Goliath, though.

" I think a lot of people, even Christians, are willing to be satisfied with gaining lots and lots of biblical knowledge— and many people go to Bible studies and don't realize it isn't enough to know what's right, it's applying the information and the knowledge that you have.

—Charles Stanley